Pathfinder

ALSO BY RON STRICKLAND

The Pacific Northwest Trail Guide
Shank's Mare
River Pigs and Cayuses
Whistlepunks and Geoducks
Vermonters
Texans
Alaskans

ABOUT THE ARTIST

Elise Zoller studied architecture at Princeton, management at Columbia, and fine arts painting at Boston's Academy of Realist Art. A graduate of Colorado Outward Bound, she has hiked parts of the Pacific Northwest Trail and other wilderness pathways. Her latest work is on display at www.elisezoller.com. Elise thanks her husband Preston and her Academy of Realist Art mentors for their support and encouragement.

Pathfinder

BLAZING A NEW WILDERNESS TRAIL IN MODERN AMERICA

Ron Strickland

Illustrations by Elise Zoller

Oregon State University Press
Corvallis

The paper in this book meets the guidelines for permanence and durability of the Committee on Production Guidelines for Book Longevity of the Council on Library Resources and the minimum requirements of the American National Standard for Permanence of Paper for Printed Library Materials Z39.48-1984.

Library of Congress Cataloging-in-Publication Data
Strickland, Ron.
  Pathfinder : blazing a new wilderness trail in modern America / Ron Strickland ; illustrations by Elise Zoller.
      p. cm.
  Includes bibliographical references and index.
  ISBN 978-0-87071-603-4 (alk. paper)
  1. Strickland, Ron. 2. Outdoor life--United States. 3. Travelers--United States--Biography. 4. Outfitters (Outdoor recreation)--United States--Biography. I. Zoller, Elise. II. Title.

  GV191.52.S77A3 2011
  796.50973--dc22

                          2010053102

First published in 2011 by Oregon State University Press
Printed in the United States of America

OSU
Oregon State
UNIVERSITY

Oregon State University Press
121 The Valley Library
Corvallis OR 97331-4501
541-737-3166 • fax 541-737-3170
http://oregonstate.edu/dept/press

To the lovely Christine "Tine" Hartmann

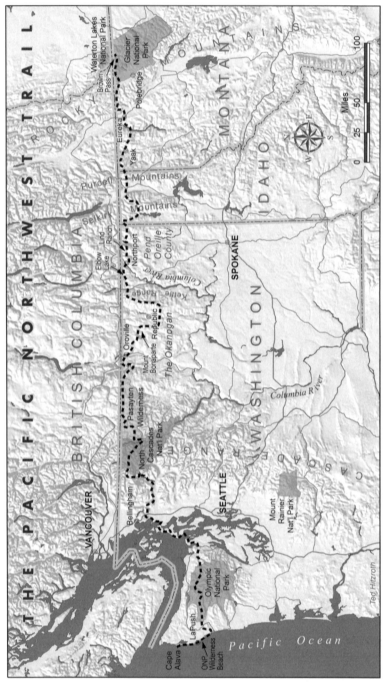

Map by Ted Hitzroth

And I'm back on the trail again,
Missed you like some long lost friend.
Sometimes I think I'm just a part of the wind,
When I'm back on the trail again.

Walkin' Jim Stoltz, "Back on the Trail Again," 1996

TABLE OF CONTENTS

Introduction

Often I can give the truest and most interesting account of
any adventure I have had after years have elapsed, for then I
am not confused, only the most significant facts surviving in
my memory.

Henry David Thoreau, *Journal* IX (1837), 311

SOME PEOPLE are just not meant to be backpackers. I used to be one of them. My golf-focused parents had no use for hiking, but even if they had been avid campers, my first experience with a tent would have taught me to be wary.

I was seven years old and a July visitor at my grandmother's beach house on Narragansett Bay in Rhode Island. Nana's neighbor boy, an eleven-year-old sophisticate named Bobby, had spent the morning playing in his pup tent with some pals. Jealous and envious little bugger that I was, I had pleaded repeatedly to join them. "No. Go away," said Bobby. All my begging had only angered him further.

But then, at noon, fate intervened. My grandmother brought out a grape jelly sandwich and ordered Bobby to show me a little hospitality. After that, it was as if the gates to explorer heaven had opened. When I crawled in with my sandwich, that canvas hut practically sang of the great outdoors. The only thing I knew that smelled that good was Dad's black four-door sedan. That car was his statement of personal pride after the shortages of the Depression and the Second World War. As I surveyed Bobby's immaculate cocoon, I shared similar feelings of well-being.

Smiling broadly with the contentment of a pint-sized *arriviste*, I pretended to camp out. The illusion was heightened by the calls of sandpipers from the nearby beach. Stretching out on one elbow, I prepared to bite into Nana's open-faced, delectable-looking sandwich. Its jelly had come from our own Concord grapes, and I

had helped to pick them. Their intense flavor was rivaled only by their rich, purple color. I was so hungry that ...

(Okay, I admit that I was a clumsy seven-year-old, but what happened next was totally unfair.)

When my sandwich landed jelly side down on that pup tent's immaculate floor, I was momentarily too stunned to react. Even today I know of no other sticky stain to rival that of the Concord grape. Invented in its eponymous town in 1849, it has defiled clothing and furniture ever since.

Pretty soon Bobby noticed that the little pest from next door had not only fouled his tent but was also trying to shovel up the purple clots with bits of bread. I think he would have hit me if he hadn't been afraid of my grandmother. Instead he dragged me out into the pitiless light of day. "I never should have let you in," he seethed. "I knew you were trouble." Offended down to the bedrock of his eleven-year-old soul, he yelled, "You ruined my tent. Scram, creep."

I have known many people whose childhood experience with a mean dog or a too-difficult hike had unfortunate, lifelong effects. After that humiliation I could easily have fallen into that pattern instead of pursuing a life of outdoor adventure.

But I did not.

PATHFINDER GREW OUT of my experiences as the founder of the 1,200-mile Pacific Northwest National Scenic Trail (PNT). Beginning in the early 1970s, I wanted to showcase the best hiking of the Rockies, Selkirks, Purcells, Okanogan, Cascades, Olympics, and Wilderness Coast. This book begins by explaining how that "fanciful" idea evolved into a Congressionally designated jewel of the National Trails System. Ultimately, however, the book is an invitation to everyone—experienced or not—to sample more of hiking's many pleasures. Walking activates all of our senses and can deliver extraordinary happiness and vitality.

Pathfinder is like a backcountry stew where the hiker chef has thrown in as many tasty ingredients as possible, not necessarily in any particular order. For instance, I delve into gear, guidebooks, and the particular pleasures of "Women on the Trail." In "Further Reading" I recommend ten books whose spirited authors would enliven any campfire. Perhaps rashly, as a person who loves trails, I even try to make sense of "The Path Ahead."

Pathfinder is also about love even though my sweetheart, the lovely Christine Hartmann, insists that there is nothing romantic about damp sleeping bags and smelly socks. I have written this book at least in part to put a little bounce into everyone's steps.

At its best, there is nothing canned or predictable about hiking. At its worst, even a face-down jelly sandwich can be part of the adventure.

I Became a Hiker Because ...

*It's not the walking I go for; it's what I find when I go. Each
and every day is fascinating. I never know what's around
the next corner. Once I came out from behind a rocky bluff
to see a magnificent stag barely ten meters away. I was close
enough to hear him breathe out in surprise. That was several
years ago, and the memory is as fresh as yesterday.*

Judy Armstrong, 2007
(after her 4,000-mile circuit of the French Southern Alps)

I NEVER SET OUT to become a professional trail developer.
As a teenager, all I ever wanted to do was fly fighter jets. When
I enrolled at Georgetown's School of Foreign Service in 1961, I'd
already spent several years as a Civil Air Patrol cadet, so it seemed
perfectly natural to join ROTC with the goal of flying F-104s.

I'd begun life as a chubby boy with short parents. To overcome
fate, I had used peanut butter as my secret weapon to grow tall.
It must have worked because in seventh grade, fueled by Skippy,
I sprouted almost overnight from five feet three inches to six feet
three inches. Yet I still weighed only 145 pounds. It was as if Nature
had extruded me through a fun house mirror. I doubt if our officers
had ever met a more ungainly recruit. Major O'Malley certainly
had a hard time finding me a flight suit at Andrews Air Force Base.
My ill-fitting helmet crimped my forehead painfully as I awaited
our orientation flight in a Shooting Star trainer.

Nevertheless, after years of devouring Battle of Britain memoirs,
I could barely hide my excitement as I slid into the rear seat next
to the ejector handle. *Dogfights, here I come*, I imagined. Major
O'Malley, as if he could read my thoughts, ordered me not to touch
my joystick.

As we took off, I felt as if I were strapped to a deafening
blowtorch. There was nothing subtle about the T-33. As the major

throttled us faster and faster down the runway, I was unable to focus on either the instruments or the fast-blurring ground. Commercial jetliners were still such a novelty that I'd never been up in a jet of any kind. But I did know enough to worry that, despite our rapid acceleration, we still hadn't risen much at all. I realized that we were accelerating in level flight toward something large and menacing at the end of the 3½-mile runway.

Major O'Malley pulled back suddenly on the stick to send the T-33 straight up into the sky like a Roman candle. Pinned against my seat, I gaped at the topsy-turvy Maryland countryside while my senses reeled and my lunch rose.

The major, a veteran of many Cold War flights above the Arctic Circle, appeared oblivious to my distress. I knew him as a terminally boring, time-serving teacher in our "military science" classes. But up here, free at last, he yawed, rolled, and dove for the sheer joy of flying. Like a puppy chasing a stick, he gamboled across the sky. Though I only saw the back of his helmet, every stomach-churning movement told me that he was as much in his element as I was out of mine. I was so startled when we burned through the atmosphere *upside down* that I scarcely breathed. As I hung from my harness, the horizon disappeared like a drink down a drunk.

Finally O'Malley remembered me and, now all business, he righted the plane, leveled off, and told me to take the controls. This was to be my moment of glory. I tried to reorient my spinning senses in order to "Fly straight toward that cloud."

"Yes, sir, I see it," I mumbled, spotting the crenellated, fluffy mass. *Nothing to it*, I thought, swallowing hard and grasping the joystick with a death grip. None of my literary aces had explained that a pilot must be like the skilled dancer who coaxes movement from his partner with a gentle hand on her back. Instead my coarse grip repeatedly sent us rocketing off course. I overcorrected like a man with bees in his flight suit. The very real joys of flight were right beneath my nose but not in my hands and brain.

Reluctantly O'Malley turned back toward Andrews. He was as eager to stay up there doing what he did best as I was anxious for my ears to stop hurting from the descent. Then to make matters worse, after our wheels touched down and I loosened my mask, I got a snootful of acrid fumes. It was all I could do to ease my wobbly legs off the wing onto the tarmac. Nauseous from the foul cockpit air and undone by the plane's aerobatics, I upchucked as soon as my boots touched ground. Major O'Malley stepped deftly aside, and gave me a disgusted look.

Later, when I flunked the red-green color-perception test, the remains of my pilot fantasy imploded. In retrospect, I realize that I was so absentminded and ill-coordinated that I should never have attempted to become a fighter pilot. But as an eighteen-year-old freshman, I knew little about my own untested character. And what I thought I knew I later learned was incorrect. It was only through dumb luck that I lived long enough to become a hiker.

AFTER MY FLYING CAREER nosedived, I lurched toward President John F. Kennedy's call to patriotic service. *Diplomatic Corps, here I come!* Imagining my future life at embassy parties, I soon affected an ascot, wore a beret, and bought a series of superannuated sports cars. Perhaps the most ridiculous part was that I didn't even know how to shift the ferocious manual transmission on my 1952 cherry red Jaguar XK-120. That exotic beast required (1) careful double clutching, (2) its own full-time

mechanic, and (3) ears of iron (to withstand the roar from its glasspack-enhanced muffler). Wherever I went the shrieking of my gears advertised my ignorance. But what did I care? I was young, and that Jag was so beautiful that some of its luster rubbed off on me as the perfect complement to my new ambassadorial persona.

Choosing a rewarding path in life is often one of the most difficult things that a person can do. My initial, stumbling efforts got me nowhere—certainly not to the State Department—even though the answer was under my feet all along.

Both flying and the Foreign Service had wanderlust in common. Perhaps I had itchy feet because I'd grown up in a New England backwater so old-fashioned that it had scarcely emerged from the nineteenth century. My mother, Winifred Gibson Strickland (1916–), and my father, Edwin Theodore "Ted" Strickland (1915–2001), were both second-generation offspring of English immigrant parents who worked in the textile mills in Rhode Island. We lived very much off the beaten path in a Cape Cod-style house where my father maintained a large vegetable garden and raised Rhode Island Red chickens. Perhaps because of lingering habits of wartime austerity, but probably because of New England frugality, Mom bottled large quantities of strawberry, grape, and raspberry jam. She put up all kinds of vegetables in Mason jars and cooked plain, unseasoned English-style meals. Each summer I tagged after her to pick high-bush blueberries on overgrown pastureland. I was little help and my four-years-younger sister, Susan, even less. But pails full at last, we were sure to feast on a juicy pie that night.

My best friend, Barton St. Armand, and I haunted a millpond trail, complete with its own little universe of bullfrogs and a rock-embedded maple known by us as the Meteor Tree. We hightailed it there every noon when the whistle blew at the textile mill. What we didn't know then was that our path would surely have led us to factory jobs if chance, ambition, and macroeconomics had not intervened.

I think Mom recognized from the beginning that education could be my ticket to a better life. At age six, I enrolled at the same

Nasonville grammar school that she'd attended in the 1920s. Kids at that bare-bones structure still used the same outdoor latrines that Mom had known. So she, to improve my prospects, transferred me to nearby Harrisville's basement-restrooms-equipped eight-room school. Our modernity was relative, though. At Harrisville Grammar School, we made our own ink from powder, kept it in desktop inkwells, and wrote with steel-nib pens that were not much of an advance from the colonial period's bird quills.

In 1955, my father moved us south to Wilmington, Delaware, to follow the dying textile industry. It was a sad uprooting for him but a lucky break for me. I became a scholarship student at Tower Hill Country Day School and embarked on a lifetime of learning.

I BECAME A HIKER because at the impressionable age of twenty I happened to read a newspaper article about a Newark, Delaware, antiques dealer who had just hiked Washington's 450-mile Cascade Crest Trail. At that point I had done little overnight hiking myself, but I was so curious that I phoned the mysterious Paris Walters (1905–1999) to request a meeting.

At the time I had never even been west of Indiana. The Sixties' political and cultural stew had begun to heat up, but I still gave the impression of having only recently fallen off the turnip truck. Ralph Waldo Emerson could have been speaking of me when he wrote:

Because I was content with these poor fields,
Low open meads, slender and sluggish streams,
And found a home in haunts which others scorned

"Ronald, come right in," purred the handsome man at the door of his antiques shop. "You are as welcome as the flowers in May." And, thus began the series of visits that continued for decades.

That first afternoon, Paris regaled me with the story of his life. I sat among his "American primitive" hutches, chests, and decoys to hear about the time he ran away from military school to join a tent show. "I played slide piano from one hick town to the next," he beamed. In a showroom redolent of linseed oil, Paris's mellow baritone evoked the jazz bands of the Roaring Twenties. He told me about his stint as a Hollywood talent scout and about his present gig selling antiques to rich collectors. Finally I found the nerve to ask about hiking.

It turned out that Paris was new to the sport himself. Less than a decade earlier, he'd been intrigued by an article about Vermont's Long Trail (LT). Completely unprepared, he'd walked half its 270-mile length until he and his nephew encountered a midnight deluge near Sherburne Pass. "As novices we didn't have wit enough to find a shelter and build a fire to dry out our sleeping bags," he said. "My nephew, who had been studying Wagnerian opera in Germany, was concerned about the condition of his vocal cords. I was wet and cold and confused. So we hopped on a bus and headed home to Delaware."

Despite that setback, Paris was so hooked on hiking that he later completed not only the Long Trail but also the Appalachian Trail and the Oregon and Washington parts of the Pacific Crest Trail. He said that his passion for the sport grew out of childhood experiences with his maternal grandfather:

> He helped open my eyes to the world of Nature: the weather, the land, and the need for food and water and shelter. He was a bark contractor for our local tannery and would often take me on his trips into the forest to buy chestnut oak bark used for tanning hides. He would plunk me up in front of the saddle and we would take off on his horse, sometimes for a week. We slept on the ground using blankets for bedrolls. Grandad always carried a frying pan, salt, lard, and a rifle for game. We more or less lived off the land: stuff like fried squirrels and morels.

During my next DC-based six years, I visited Paris whenever I returned to Delaware. He always urged me to go west to hike, but I needed a major catastrophe to make me do it. On April 4,

1968, the assassination of Martin Luther King, Jr., set off days of pandemonium as two hundred fires burned simultaneously. Things were so bad that it took 13,600 federal troops three days to reclaim the city from thousands of rioters. Thirteen people died; over a thousand were injured. I was eager to escape the mayhem.

Even if there hadn't been a racial insurrection, any DC summer, before the advent of air conditioning, was enough to make my spirits sink. Also my twenty-two-year-old girlfriend was way too eager to follow her recently married friends to the altar. I wanted none of that, especially when what I considered to be "the real America" beckoned from out beyond the Beltway.

1968 was a watershed year for America and, I hoped, for me. However, I was unsure what to do until Paris Walters offered me advice that appealed to my deepest instincts. "Ronald," he drawled, "why don't you take the summer off to hike the Cascade Crest Trail like I did? You're young. There's nothing holding you back."

In 1968, the North Cascades Mountains offered some of the grandest roadless hiking in the Lower Forty-Eight. When I got off the bus one chilly day at Snoqualmie Pass, I mentally thanked Paris Walters for the 250 miles of wilderness that awaited me on my walk north to Canada.

Following sketchy maps, I immediately felt like an ant among the U-shaped valleys and jagged peaks. The Cascade Crest had a raw, unfinished quality; work crews were still blasting new sections of the trail from solid rock. Steaming piles of bear scat hinted at hidden danger. But there was music in the creeks and snow on the summits. I didn't care that I sometimes went comically astray. It was enough to have escaped DC's heat, humidity, pollution, and political chaos. I may have been a greenhorn, but I began to feel with each new mile that at last I was getting somewhere.

I climbed slowly past Snow Lake, a deep bowl ringed by 100-foot old-growth Douglas firs (whose tiny cones seemed altogether too small for such magnificent trees). Literally awash in new sensations, I soaked in a sun-splashed, fern-bedecked hot spring that emerged from an old mine shaft. The otherworldly sounds of varied thrushes lent a fairytale quality to the astonishing forest and its magical mine.

That enchanted feeling guided my steps all the way north to the international frontier. The first half of the hike required many thousands of feet of elevation gain and loss as the trail wound over passes, through glacier-carved valleys, and along ridges. The second half, wilder still, challenged and amazed me with rugged mountains, a dormant volcano, and permanent snowfields. Most days there was water in the sky, water underfoot, and drizzle down my neck. Even when rain was not actually falling, thick mists kept the brush (and me) soaked. As a result, I only had glimpses of the long panoramas that Paris had promised. Except for those brief sun breaks, I had to content myself with the unexpected charm of mushrooms, flowers, toads, and mosses. Then, whenever I became too contemplative, a grouse was always sure to pop my reverie by bursting noisily from its hiding place.

DURING THE FIRST couple of days I thought more about pain than the landscape's grandeur. I'd bussed in directly from sea level at Seattle to Snoqualmie Pass to hike at elevations of as much as 7,000 feet. The combination of that altitude plus a 65-pound pack meant that I was chronically out of breath. Skinny as I was at sixfeet three inches and 150 pounds, my load weighed almost half as much as I did. It contributed to the merciless bastinado that I suffered from rocks, roots, and my tight, inflexible boots.

In 1968, I was too green to realize that Paris's hiking methods hadn't evolved much from the era of the fur trappers. So, imitating him, I hauled along a rubber poncho that produced so much sweat that I needn't have bothered trying to stay dry. My 5-pound sleeping bag kept me warm at night but was outrageously heavy. The tube tent that Paris had recommended was an 8-foot-long, open-ended, plastic pillowcase that ripped easily and condensed readily. If I'd been even a little bit wiser, I would have substituted a lightweight tarp and a ground cloth.

Paris's worst recommendation stemmed from the fact that he was so fastidious and dandified that he never liked to go unshaven. He weighed me down with a 2-pound can of whisker foam. When I awoke after my first day of hiking, every part of my tall, skinny body protested against my dangerously heavy load. I hurt from my toes to my shoulders. Even the gray matter between my ears would have throbbed if there'd been more of it.

After disconsolately spreading minty goo on my face and taking a few swipes with the razor, I abandoned the whole shitteree right there next to a boulder where the next fool could find it. From that moment on, I wore the resulting scraggly beard with misplaced pride. In photographs taken during the next thirteen years my face resembles the hide of a mangy coyote.

I also had Paris Walters to thank for my gaseous menus. "Cooking in the woods is easy," he advised. "Just boil water, add split pea soup mix, and thicken it with cornmeal and bits of compressed bacon." Paris actually bragged that his yellow-green, primordial slop would make anyone "fart like a bull." No wonder that my bowels often competed for sympathy with my aching feet, legs, lungs, and back.

Clothes were another sore point. "Gay Paree," as he often called himself, invariably sported stylish summer duds. Following his fashion dictates, I was usually so chilled from rain, hail, and snow that I had to move fast just to keep warm. Thanks to him, I was always on the verge of hypothermia.

Yet young as I was, I never cared that my gear failed repeatedly. Each morning I hoisted my pack with new confidence. Every day my strength grew. A week out, and I strode along like I knew what I was doing. Backpacking all day, every day, I felt stronger by the hour. Finally one giddy evening, hiking by the moon, my T-shirt steamed in an otherworldly light. Pure animal exuberance surged through my veins. I had never felt so free and so alive to the moment.

Throughout that trip my predominant feeling was joy. That was especially true during the final forty miles. Periodically reprieved from the oppression of squalls and sleet, I gaped as views piled atop views. Glaciers, lakes, and peaks kept coming and coming and coming. And if that weren't enough, I often stumbled upon wildlife that literally stopped me in my tracks. I remember crossing an alpine pass where black bears, mountain goats, birds, and rodents (pikas, conies, and marmots) hinted at the ecological richness of pre-Columbian America.

That North Cascades summer unlocked something in me that had been struggling to get out. I became a hiker because in navigating the wilderness I discovered a new direction for my life. I loved trails because they were the most exciting things I'd ever experienced. Opportunity appeared out of the fog, and I found my path.

My mother always blamed Paris Walters for my "failure" to follow her advice to become a Fortune 500 CEO or a Wall Street heavyweight. "If it hadn't been for that bum," she used to say, "you could have amounted to something." But I became a hiker because the North Cascades made me happy.

Paris used to delight in telling about how he met the first woman to thru-hike the Appalachian Trail. He said:

In May 1963, I was walking along the trail in Shenandoah National Park when I glanced ahead and saw an old woman headed my way. She was wearing a hat, tennis shoes, and a homemade plastic raincoat. A bundle was tied around her waist. Oh, she was so wild looking that I knew without being told that she was the Queen of the Appalachian Trail, Grandma Gatewood. I had heard so much about this woman, what she wore and how she traveled, that I almost felt that I knew her. She walked the entire trail twice and was known and welcomed from one end to the other. She was asked into more homes for the night than George Washington ever was. When I met her, Grandma was walking several hundred miles from Pennsylvania to

Roan Mountain, North Carolina, to see the rhododendrons in bloom. Knowing of her experience through all sections of the Trail, I asked her which part she liked best. "Going downhill, Sonny," she replied.

Grandma Gatewood had it right. There was nothing complicated about hiking. And its simplicity and deep immersion in Nature were just what I needed.

The Bad Boys of Backpacking

Once the Trail [Study] bill has been passed by Congress, I
plan to let Northwesterners take up the cause; I'll move on
to something else. Because of my efforts here in Washington,
political support for the Trail has outdistanced grassroots
work on the project ... The next group of Trail workers
must begin where I leave off. You see, I keep thinking of the
example of the Appalachian Trail, fifty years old this year,
which succeeded because of the dedicated volunteers all up
and down the East Coast.

Letter from the author to Harvey Manning
May 5, 1975, Washington, DC

IN AMERICA'S recreational trails world, the gold standard for mega-routes is congressional designation. According to the 1968 National Trails System Act, *national scenic trails* are "extended trails so located as to provide for maximum outdoor recreation potential and for the conservation and enjoyment of nationally significant scenic, historic, natural, and cultural qualities of the area through which such trails may pass." In 1970, there were only two official national scenic trails, the Appalachian and the Pacific Crest, both designated by the 1968 Act. If anyone wishes to add a trail to the system, he or she must persuade Congress to pass legislation that mandates creation of a federal study of the new route's "feasibility and desirability." If that report is favorable, Congress must pass (1) a second bill to endorse the project and (2) subsequent bills to fund and develop it in cooperation with relevant public and private entities. All told, that process is so arduous that only a very stubborn sort of foolish dreamer would attempt it. Maybe that was why I succeeded where so many other smarter folks failed.

17

In early 1970, while a political science grad student at Georgetown, I came across a book about the new North Cascades National Park. Conservationist Harvey Manning's large-format photo volume was "an invitation to come enjoy—and then help save." He ended by fantasizing about a cross-Cascades hike that would be "a month to remember." After reading its place names, I could think of nothing else.

Romantic twenty-something that I was, I daydreamed constantly about trails instead of concentrating on my ongoing graduate

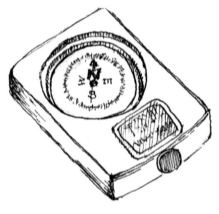

studies. Unbelievable as it seems to me now, I went AWOL from grad school in the summers of 1970–1973 to begin piecing together an east-west route from Montana, through Idaho to Washington, using everything from bushwhacks to unmaintained/abandoned pathways and drovers' tracks. Those hikes were an order of magnitude more arduous than anything I'd ever attempted, but I soon believed that they had the potential to coalesce into a superb new entity that I called the Pacific Northwest Trail.

Hiking is one thing, and flunking out is another. I combined my desire for a trail and for a doctorate by researching the politics of how Congress had created new official wilderness areas after the 1964 passage of the Wilderness Act. Like most dissertations, mine made no ripples in the wider world. However, its real significance was that it inspired me to attempt to add the Pacific Northwest Trail to the National Trails System. In the late spring of 1974, I blithely wrote a study bill and set about finding a congressman to introduce it. I was too inexperienced to worry that the hitherto unknown project lacked any local support in the three states through which it ran.

I did, however, pester fellow DC environmentalists and my Seattle friends for help. That included Randolph Urmston, a high school classmate who had moved to Seattle to practice law. On the night that he hosted a Young Republicans meeting, I cornered the speaker, Frank Pritchard, to give him an earful about the trail. One thing led to another; he put me in touch with his brother, Seattle congressman Joel Pritchard, who later introduced my bill as H.R. 15298. And to make a long story short, in 1976, a few months after I finished my doctorate, Congress passed our PNT "study bill" legislation.

I had already devoted much of the previous eight years to locating routes, lobbying bigwigs, raising funds, and forming a PNT club. To me the trail was already a viable, going concern—and four young Oregonians had recently thru-hiked every inch of it.

In 1978, when a federal study team began a study of the PNT's "feasibility and desirability," I was fully confident that they would urge Congress to add the trail to the National Trails System. Once again my naivete won out over common sense. I failed to consider that the PNT was still merely a *concept* that lacked signs, blazes, and, sometimes, even tread. What was worse, its shaky *political* facade was about to collapse around my ears.

I had been a wilderness activist throughout graduate school, but somehow I had never noticed that trails were of little or no interest to Seattle's conservation groups. Though Eastern trail clubs maintained hundreds of miles of trails as a public service, the analogous Seattle Mountaineers maintained none. For the latter's climbing- and preservation-oriented leaders, trails had been unimportant; their great battles had been to create the North Cascades National Park, establish wilderness areas, and defeat logging, mining, and grazing. The prevailing Northwest sentiment was that trails were the responsibility of the Forest Service, not hikers.

I was such a complete outsider (I didn't move to the Northwest from DC until autumn of 1977) that I was genuinely surprised by preservation leaders' hostility to even the long-established Pacific Crest Trail. It was inconceivable to me that they believed that the PNT "would be even worse" than the PCT. In fact, the head of the Olympic Park Associates, Polly Dyer, complained in the *Seattle Weekly*: "This [PNT] legislation was going through Congress without any of the Northwest organizations who are very concerned about trails—especially where it affects wilderness—being aware of it ... We don't want to see another PCT, which is a trunk line trail, three feet, four feet wide." The North Cascades Conservation Council's president, Patrick Goldsworthy, actually told *The Seattle Weekly* that national designation of the PNT would be a "kind of curse."

I should have anticipated this clique's reaction because of an earlier incident involving an eighteen-year-old Midwestern thru-hiker. In 1971, *The High Adventure Of Eric Ryback* exploded into print during America's generational earthquakes of the civil rights era, the Vietnam War, and the sexual revolution. Soon even non-hikers grooved to the teen's tale of walking from Canada to Mexico on the Pacific Crest Trail. Eric Ryback became a cultural hero to his peers, and for a few wonderful years backpacking was "in" as hiker fashions went mainstream.

However, Seattle's Old Guard conservationists were horrified by the influx of longhairs into their bailiwick. Instead of applauding Ryback, they excoriated him for exaggerating the number of miles he had walked. Looking back, I feel that the furor was more about who the teen was than about the distance he did or did not hike. Eric Ryback's real sins in provincial Seattle were (1) that he was an outsider who had not taken the Mountaineers' Climbing Course and (2) that he had the effrontery to mention what they considered to be *their area* in his book. In short, he was both an example and a cause of the tides of change that swept across the region.

Though I recognize that the teenager may possibly have inflated his mileage totals, the essential fact is that *High Adventure* was ahead of its time in publicizing the joys of long-distance hiking. Its author was and is a thru-hiking pioneer and hero.

During the 1970s, the neologism *Rybacker* was commonly used as an epithet in Seattle. I know, because it increasingly bounced off my own hide. The trouble began so gradually that I, like a lobster in a warming pot, never worried that things were about to get very hot. In late April 1977, my PNT friends and I were stunned by a statement from the North Cascades Conservation Council (N3C). The group proclaimed itself to be "inalterably opposed to the routing of an officially designated 'Pacific Northwest Trail' anywhere within the boundaries of the Pasayten Wilderness Area and the North Cascades National Park." The trail, N3C said, would "attract more users than the resource can withstand." Like the Pacific Crest Trail, the PNT would siphon off funding from the "construction and maintenance of more needed trails" elsewhere. Also:

> As has been shown by the example of the Pacific Crest Trail, a "national scenic trail" is constructed to high standards inconsistent with the National Wilderness Preservation System. Such construction imposes irreversible damage on the wilderness resource and detracts from the wilderness experience of the visitor.

I was saddened that anyone would equate the Pacific Northwest Trail with environmental rapine. And I felt certain that the May 1, 1978, public hearing would correct that misunderstanding.

How could I have been so wrong?

Speaking on behalf of our trail club, Janet Garner, twenty-one, told the large gathering about her experiences thru-hiking the PNT the previous summer. I thought she made a good case for the trail's present joys and future benefits. However, the angry crowd emphatically disagreed. Over a hundred people rose in righteous indignation to denounce the devilish project. At six subsequent regional hearings, most speakers echoed the arguments of the N3C. One seer, incongruously wearing pajamas, even suggested that the trail would bring a flood of litterbugs whose broken bottles would cut the feet of passing deer.

The hearings were a rout. Never even bothering to research my laboriously developed route, the Study Team echoed the N3C's position that the trail would ruin the environment, siphon funds from more deserving trails, and cost over $100 million for land acquisition. The team's report recommended against further federal consideration. Case closed. The Pacific Northwest Trail was officially dead.

I ADMIT THAT I was mostly to blame for that disastrous outcome. In retrospect, I should have known better than to begin the legislative process without building a powerful grassroots coalition. Well, the bottom line was that after the Study Team fiasco, there were only two choices: give up or take radical action.

I have never been a quitter. As the 1980s began, I continued to be inspired by the example of the Appalachian Trail. I had corresponded with and admired Benton MacKaye, its founder, and I knew many AT volunteers. But what could I do?

I knew that one of the Study Team's most egregious lies was that PNT land acquisition would cost at least $100 million (in 1979 dollars). So my few fellow conspirators and I decided to fight back by physically building the trail for free and out of sight of our Seattle opponents. In other words, like certain notorious, Vietnam-era groups, we went underground. From then on the PNT became at least metaphorically an outlaw trail.

LOOKING BACK ON IT, I was too young and inexperienced to realize that my cause was most probably lost. The federal study had gone decisively against the trail. I was so penurious that I lived in a $40/month University District boarding house where I focused all of my energy on the project. The cash-strapped Pacific Northwest Trail Association was nonprofit; I was unpaid. Also, if I were to continue with my pipe dream, I needed to construct a demonstration section to prove the PNT's feasibility, but I had never built an inch of trail in my life. Could anything have been more hopeless?

My buddy, Port of Seattle engineer Larry Reed, suggested that I drive down to Mt. Rainier to seek help at the Boy Scouts of America's Camp Sheppard. Its sixty-six-year-old chief ranger Max

Eckenburg (1916–2001), had already located and constructed hundreds of miles of trails using Scout labor. Luckily for me, I arrived at a time when he was eager for a new challenge. And it just so happened that he had already tangled with a PNT opponent who more than twenty years earlier had fought Tacoma Mountain Rescue's efforts to build a rescue hut two-thirds of the way up Mount Rainier. Max and his Mountain Rescue pals had hauled steel plates up there, built Camp Schurman, and thus saved many lives. Luckily for me, that history predisposed Max to be *very* eager to join the bad boys of backpacking.

Max was old and broke. I was young and broke. But we were also sneaky and determined. During the winter of 1982–1983, we made multiple scouting trips each week to Samish Bay's dramatic, seaside hills north of Seattle to choose a route for our PNT demonstration project. Everything was against us. But we were too stubborn to give up.

Along the PNT: North Cascades

*It was the middle of the night, but we had to continue out
of there quickly to try to get over Hannegan Pass before the
Chilliwack Trail was snowed in for the winter.*

Max Eckenburg, interview with the author, 1983

SALISH SEA PRECIPITATION, at lowland elevations, is a steady
diet of swirling mists, diaphanous fogs, and shifting curtains of
blowing spume. Without it we would not have our world-class
Douglas firs, western red cedars, and true firs. And where would we
be without the damp earth smells of ferns and mosses? The scent of
our rain varies: there is the rain-of-the-heights smell and the rain-
of-the-valley smell. Puget Sound weather is so unpredictable and
so prone to Scotch mists because we live in the midst of converging
rivers of air. Then there are our "one-hundred-year storms" that
every few winters disrupt commerce, increase the birth rate, and
sometimes sink bridges.

Drizzle restores waterways and greenery; one of the best places
on the Pacific Northwest Trail to appreciate this is in North
Cascades National Park. To be honest I might as well call it *Rain*
National Park and drop the more poetic word *Cascades*. Anywhere
from the sere Okanogan westward is mighty moist. And dyed-in-
the-wool Puget Sounders like it that way.

One of my favorite rivers, the Upper Chilliwack, runs gray/
green with glacial silt. Curving north into Canada, it eventually
becomes part of the mighty Fraser River. For decades PNT hikers
crossed the wild Chilliwack's corridor-in-the-firs in a metal basket.

Note: I have interspersed a series of PNT vignettes throughout
this book in order to share some of the trail's many places and
people. These mini-adventures are directional signs to some of the
PNT magic that is often only a few steps away, around the next
switchback.

I, suspended beneath a steel cable, have happily pulled myself in that swaying contraption across to the far shore. Inevitably, half way over, I stopped above the turbulent river when I heard a gruff, familiar voice. "Never can a packer, Ron, at the end of the season."

That was Max Eckenburg talking to me across the years about the job he'd had near that spot at the Forest Service's administrative and communication center, US Cabin. In 1941, Max, then twenty-five years old, was boss of the area's Forest Service trail crew. At the end of the season, he fired his horse packer for animal cruelty. That meant that Max (who was not a horseman) had to load up the horses and pack out the trail crew's voluminous trail maintenance equipment all by himself. That was difficult enough. But it was November and there were twelve wilderness miles to go from Indian Creek to Hannegan Pass. So much snow had already fallen that Max was afraid that he was about to be trapped down in the remote valley.

Indian Creek Camp was 4¼ miles downstream from US Cabin, on the opposite (east) side of the river. As Max explained it to me,

I was down there alone with this seven-horse pack string, cleaning up stuff and getting ready to come out. Hannegan Pass was the only way out on the American side of the border. But when you get a foot and a half of early snow laying all over the place and then you get a warm Chinook rain, that stuff's gonna come out of there like flushing a toilet. And, boy, they flushed it on me that night! [Laughter] It was a real bugger!

Well, it rained and it rained, and that snow began to melt all through that watershed. The river kept rising until I finally made up my mind that, hey, if I was going to go, I'd better go.

By the time I got the horses packed, the river was roaring from one side of the valley to the other, all down through those low woods. Of course, you could usually see sand

there, which meant that the valley floor flooded from time to time. In fact, we even built our shelters down there on stilts so the water could run underneath.

Anyway about an hour after dark I started out of there on the horses. I couldn't wait until the next day because by then that water would be too deep in the valley. And if the rain turned to snow at the pass, the trail would be impassable. So I had to leave in the dark. There was no choice. It was getting worse by the hour.

Well, here we were trying to cross the Chilliwack above Indian Creek, and the horses were just skipping along out in the river. Their feet barely touched here and there. And the lead horse King (that I was riding) stopped. Right out there in the bloody water! And he was not quite being lifted and pushed downstream.

I turned on my headlamp and here was a whole dang tree going by!

So King kept stopping, and then he'd go ahead. It was pitch black. Just raining and blowing horizontal and all that debris in the river. Oh God, one tree in the middle of that seven-horse string and you can see where I'd be. Oh, we were living by the skin of our teeth!

When we finally got across we found that the trail on the north side had washed out. It was gone!

But there was an old trail above that one because the lower one had washed out before in years gone by. King remembered where that old trail was! So up through the huckleberries we went.

That son of a gun! I just gave him free rein because King knew more about the terrain than I did. He'd been down in there eighteen years.

Then the minutes went by, and the half hours went by. And the dang hours went by. The whole thing from the time I left Indian Creek till I got up to the cabin probably was three hours. But it seemed like a week because there was so much happening.

So finally I just hung onto that saddle and dozed off. Not asleep but hunched over and staying just as warm as I could. [Laughter] I was wondering how long this was going to go on.

Finally, why, King stopped and everything was quiet. I gave him a little nudge to keep going but he wouldn't budge. Then I began to come alive a little bit. I turned on my headlamp and I was looking right at the eaves of US Cabin. And just inside that was the door to where the oats were. And that's where King was planning to stay. [Laughter]

So I just got off and hugged him. I just felt like kissing him right on the lips, ya know, because without him in that mess … Oh, I tell ya!

But after I fed the horses and got something to eat myself, I began to feel cold again. It was the middle of the night, but we had to continue out of there quickly to try to get over Hannegan Pass before the Chilliwack Trail was snowed in for the winter.

Four or five hours later we got through Hell's Gulch just before daylight. The snow was really coming down. God, I got up there in the big open meadows of Hannegan Basin where we had tripods that held up our phone lines off the ground in great big sweeps of wire. The snow was already a foot and a half deep when we stopped for a break at Hannegan Shelter.

It was daylight and snowing like a bugger when we started up on the final mile to the pass. Just before I started up the final switchbacks, a mare went down on her back, all tangled up in No. 9 telephone wire. She had a couple of bad cuts and, oh, what a mess.

So I said, boy, I'm gonna leave that doggone load. I'm not going to try to repack that horse if I can get the load off her and free her from that wire. So I got in there with the pliers which I always carried and cut the wire away and I left that load.

Well, it was getting to the point where just a few minutes were going to make the difference. Up toward the top the horses were lunging. I mean when the snow gets deep enough a horse is going to lunge. He's got to.

Now I had no feeling in my hands.

But just as I got over the top of the pass, here came the guys from the ranger station. They were coming in because they knew I was in trouble.

And so we went back with one horse and got that load and brought it on up. And we got everything out to the road by dark that second night.

Ron, that whole thing started just because I canned a packer. And I canned him because of cruelty. But it backfired on me.

When I look back at that night, there was a lot of luck. But the only reason I came through at all was because I had a horse down there who after eighteen years knew where all the old trails were. He'd been through some of those high waters before. He was just fantastic.

Crossing the river, finding a trail, and bucking that snow, all in the dark, that night was a bugger! [Laughter.] I tell you, I made up my mind I'd never can a packer just before the end of the season again. No matter what!

A trail is sometimes not just a footpath but also a hint of the people who have passed ahead of us. Hiking tells me that history is underfoot wherever I walk.

In the great chain of snowy mountains east of the Salish Sea, the many forms of precipitation fall on the peaks and forests like a benediction. Ferns and mosses drip with dew. Firs grow to outrageous heights, and stories pass from person to person like bursts of sunshine.

Bucking the Brush

*Ron, if you wait for the sun to shine in this country, you'll
never go out.*

Max Eckenburg, Chief Trail Locator
Pacific Northwest Trail Association, 1983

IN 1982, EAGER TO RESURRECT the Pacific Northwest Trail
after the federal Study Team pronounced it dead on arrival, I had
come up with the unorthodox plan of trying to build the PNT as
an "outlaw trail." Because cross-country exploration would be
essential, I sought out the ready smile and crushing handshake
of the aforementioned Max Eckenburg. In his black beret, red
suspenders, logger boots, and thick woolens, he looked woodsy
enough to grow moss. Max had a reputation for straight talk and
measurable progress. His trail-locating experience dated back to
the Great Depression. But, and this was a big but, did someone
twenty-seven years my senior still have the strength to get out in
the wilds? After all, he was so ancient that he'd been the draftsman
who'd designed the "crapper" in the B-17 World War II bomber.
And in 1983 he was inching toward retirement from his latest
career as a boys' camp ranger. What would he be like to work
with? Who was he really?

The basic story was simple enough. His father had driven
"saddlebag" steam locomotives when our section of Skagit County
was railroad logged. Max's family was poor, and he joined the
Civilian Conservation Corps in the 1930s to help bring in money.
But there was something else. From the beginning it seemed that
he combined practical woods skills with a high level of moral
indignation. For instance, in 1937 he quit a pioneering thru-hike
of the Pacific Crest Trail because he was angry that his hiking
partner had gotten a girl pregnant. And, even more amazing, he
had quit junior college rather than look the other way when a

teacher let students cheat on exams. (Max spent the rest of his life resenting "four-year degree" men.) Most puzzling of all, I sensed that though he was an inspirational figure to generations of boys, he was alienated from his own kids.

Over time I learned that Max's mile-wide streak of rigidity and stubbornness was overlain with great generosity of spirit. In short, he was the ideal person to be my chief co-conspirator.

IN CHOOSING THE LOCATION for a new trail, the first thing to know is that every inch of ground, however wild looking, belongs to somebody. For our proposed route beside Samish Bay, that somebody was the Washington Department of Natural Resources (DNR). So I sought permission to build what DNR called a "scratch trail" (i.e., a glorified game trail). I doubt that I could have persuaded the agency's woodsy officials without my friends' good-old-boy credentials. They—Larry Reed (Scouting and engineering) and Pat Cummins (forestry)—did all the talking whenever we visited tin hat fellahs whose cheeks were full of snoose. My Eastern accent was so suspect with such "timber beasts" that I always relied for credibility on, for example, Max's tales about the pranks his old foreman Blackie Burns used to play on the guys in the bunkhouse.

After obtaining DNR's permission, the next step was to locate a way down to Samish Bay from a North Cascades outlier range known as the Chuckanut Mountains. Our access to saltwater was restricted by DNR's minuscule waterfront ownership and by a forested escarpment so steep and high that hang gliders, a decade later, would use its winds for uplift.

"Steep as a cow's face," is how Max put it. I remember the first time that any of us followed him into the brush on Blanchard "Hill," where drizzle's sweet caress embraced the ferns, and the smell of the Salish Sea mixed with the scent of fir. Leaving the grade of an overgrown logging railway, we tried to keep up with the old ranger as he charged through the woods like a Chuckanut gorilla.

Though he was only medium height, his square build and size $7^1/_2$ EEEEE logger boots made him seem larger. From time to time he let out a whoop when he found a rusty cable (a "Washington iron snake") or some other memento of the logging railroad.

Only my relative youthfulness—I was thirty-nine—enabled me to keep up with the old-timer whenever he disappeared into the ferns, blackberries, and ocean spray. Though he complained about his stiff back, he slipped effortlessly along game trails and through natural openings in the scree, ravines, and thickets. Following him, I began to earn my degree in "bucking the brush."

Over the next ten years, off and on, we located trail across steep, convoluted country from sea level at Samish Bay to about 4,000 feet on Mount Josephine, sixty-four miles to the east. The landscape was a crazy quilt of overgrown clearcuts, impassable swamps, briar-choked hellholes, and gigantic second-growth fir. The ownership boundaries in those sixty-four miles were as confusing as the bugs were voracious.

By correlating his course, elapsed time, and memorized 80-foot contours, Max always seemed to know where we were. Though he pulled out his hand-drawn map occasionally to explain things to me, he might just as well have left it at home because he needed it so little for his own purposes.

My job during each reconnaissance was to mark our passage with blue-and-white-striped surveyor's tape. Pretty soon colorful ribbons laced our slopes until we knew Blanchard Hill's every smile and dimple. "That's learning the country," Max beamed.

We learned each other's quirks, too. Max was so stubborn that, true to the "traditional Scout way," he refused to drink any water during our outings. As a result he sometimes suffered such severe leg cramps that he had to lie on the ground until the pain passed. The first time that happened, I thought he was dying. Of course, I realized that his self-inflicted dehydration was foolish. But even if I could have talked him out of it, I'm not sure if I would really have wanted to change anything about Max Eckenburg. To this day I

still burst out with *bon mot* "Maxims" whenever I talk with people who knew him.

I was ever the Eastern greenhorn and he the master woodsman. He accorded me pretend deference as the project's "four-year degree" straw boss while I looked to him to play the favorite uncle role, especially concerning campcraft. For instance, Max loved to anticipate what we would do if forced to bivouac overnight out in the back of beyond. "We'll use my axe to build a warming fire against a boulder," he promised gleefully, "and hunker down under a tent tree." His recourse in any situation was sure to be his Hudson's Bay cruiser axe, honed to scalpel sharpness.

By contrast, I carried a Woodsman's Pal, an odd cross between a machete and a pruning hook. I loved that thing until the day that Max derided it as "East Coast." He added that I had no more idea about axemanship "than a cub bear knows how to fondle his dick." He was overjoyed later when the brush swallowed my louche Pal, forcing me to buy a real axe at a garage sale.

My Silva sighting compass was much more redemptive—unless I forgot to bring it. Then I was sure to hear, "Never go into the woods, Ron, without your compass! It can save your life." The two tools I used most, though, were Max's clinometer (a slope measurement tool) and his 110-foot steel surveying tape. Our trail-location bushwhacks sought the ideal combination of features, directness, and grade for our stealth trail. It was not enough to walk through once or twice and then start chopping and digging. No, first Max had to sit at his salvaged-from-Boeing drafting table to manually redraw our fifteen-minute map to a scale of twelve inches to the mile. Then after innumerable reconnoitering trips, we measured the final route in 110-foot increments by slinking the tape through the ferns and tules. I recorded each of those segments' azimuth and angle of rise or fall in a yellow rainproof cruiser's book. Later Max plotted the figures onto his big chart. To my amazement, over a distance of several miles, his advancing pencil line mapped out exactly right. "That's just craphouse luck," he beamed. But I knew better because each of our lengthy shortcuts across new country arrived at our destination with astounding accuracy.

An additional complication was the need to maintain a 10 percent or less average grade. Max said he'd borrowed that rule from the Roman legions. "If it was good enough for Julius Caesar," he said, "it will be good enough for the Pacific Northwest Trail." Greenhorn that I was, I never realized that Max over-engineered our pathway the same way that he'd probably over-designed his B-17 toilet.

When we began working in November 1982, Blanchard Hill's jumbled terrain was a maze of both 100-foot-tall second-growth Doug firs and dog fur alders. Often we found the charred hulks of long-dead cedar monsters, which we sometimes cut into marker stakes. Solid as new wood, their perfume clung to us all day.

By hammering in a stake every few feet, Max sculpted the tread into and away from the slope, over and around obstacles. Switchbacks were a special concern because on our steep, erodible pitches we had to design turns that the public could not shortcut. Our goal throughout was to obtain a tread eighteen inches wide over which a horse and rider could safely pass.

We cached our tools under a hidden tarp where the view of Mount Rainier, Samish Bay, the Olympic Mountains, and the San Juan Islands made us forget our aches, scratches, and doubts. Sometimes, rather than return south to Seattle, we stayed the night. After the last traces of the orange sun dropped beyond the San Juan Islands, familiar stars emerged above Saddlebag Island. Up and down the coast, the lights of towns and cities glowed like constellations. Far to the south, Puget Sound's unseen megalopolis gave off an unnatural glow.

Part of my role was to record sequences of 110-foot segments that snaked between the crumbling bark of Blanchard Hill's mammoth stumps. Sometimes I yelled for help after I landed upside down in a briar-choked pit. Whatever happened, I always felt Max's joy to be out in the blowdowns, bugs, and sleet. In that vertiginous, broken country, he could always sense the pleasure that future hikers would feel at a split boulder, a picturesque stump, or a marine panorama. He used to say, "Ron, this trail will be so good that I could take my grandmother up it in a wheelchair."

Today the Blanchard Hill section that he designed is his much-loved memorial. But if I close my eyes, his black beret, red suspenders, and tattered mackinaw are still up ahead, plunging into the devil's club and ocean spray. I'm tagging along, happily tying surveyor tape onto fir boughs as we push deeper and deeper into the brush.

Of course, heaven help me if I've left my axe at home. Then I'll be sure to hear, "Never go into the woods, Ron, without your axe. It can save your life."

Ralph Thayer's Broadaxe

Before there was a road here I located all these trails from
the main river trail up pretty near every crick. Alone.
Ralph Thayer, 1978, interview with the author

PART OF THE REASON I love hiking is its many opportunities to hear great stories. In the early 1970s, guidebook guru Harvey Manning told me, "The *people* you have met! Personally, I have never met so damn many people as you have hiking this same country." Harvey also called me a lollygagger for stopping to talk to *everybody* on the PNT.

Beginning with trail stories, I segued into writing oral history books. The more folksy a story was, the more I loved it, as when Paris Walters told me about using his first indoor toilet. "They set me on that thing," he said, remembering his terror, "and the water came shooting through there and nearly scared the bejesus out of me."

Back when I began to develop the PNT, I was especially talkative because palavers were part of my way of learning the country. "Where are you headed?" I always asked trail travelers. "Have far have you come?" For instance, it was only after meeting a hiker from Chesaw that I first thought about routing the trail across north-central Washington's beautiful, must-see, roadless mountains. Today the Kettle Range is one of the PNT's most popular sections.

In those early PNT-development seasons, I decided to work out the PNT's route from the North Fork of the Flathead River to the town of Eureka, Montana. So I made a point of seeking out famed trails locator Ralph Thayer (1890–1983). I was so intent upon getting his advice that I scarcely noticed the craftsmanship that he'd poured into his 1912 cabin. Which of his routes, I wondered, would Ralph recommend that I use to connect the North Fork to the next valley to the west?

Still tall and straight at the age of eighty-eight, the former Forest Service timber cruiser was touchingly pleased that I was interested in his long-ago work. However, his sister, visiting from Minnesota, was so pushy that weak, diffident Ralph could scarcely get a word in edgeways. Luckily another visitor diverted her to the back room so that Ralph and I could talk uninterruptedly.

We sat beside the old homesteader's wood stove and examined the yellowed map on which, in the 1920s, he had sketched the new trails that he located up the drainages into the ranges just west of the North Fork. Since I had never interviewed anyone before, I let my host carry the conversation. Whenever I had a question, I bided my time to ask it until after I understood what he was trying to get across. In other words, instead of blurting out my own experiences, I focused on his.

I genuinely wanted Ralph Thayer's advice. Later, after I had done hundreds of such interviews, I realized that a conservative questioning style was the key to productive oral history questioning. In fact, as I wrote long ago, "Listening is not as easy as it looks. It takes infinite patience. Most of all the listener must care. It is an art of subtle encouragement. In a roomful of people the happiest person is to be found beside a good listener."

Although I had sought out Ralph for advice about routes for the PNT, our talk became so much more than that. Pretty soon the conversation drifted to a description of how Ralph had cut, peeled, and raised his cabin's logs. I learned that he had also built part of the mercantile in Polebridge. "The marks of my broadaxe still show on those ceiling beams," he said proudly. A broadaxe, by the way, is exactly what its name implies—a wide-headed chopper that is used to hew a flat surface onto a log. In this case, Ralph used it to ensure that his cabin's inside walls and beams would be flat. Knowing how to wield a broadaxe was one of Ralph's many homesteading skills, which also included weaving moose-hide snowshoes.

I was impressed with his independence and fortitude. It was obvious from his tales that Ralph had spent a lot of time by himself in the woods. "I located all these trails," he said, "from the main river trail up pretty near every crick. Alone." There weren't even any *roads* when he first started locating trails after World War I. Ralph's job was to pioneer the way for trail-building crews from the river up into the mountains. He averaged ten miles a day blazing new trail cross-country. "I had to run a rough preliminary first," he said. "Five, six, or eight or so miles, from the starting point at the main trail on the river. Climbing all the time. Sometimes I'd have to go over it twice to see which way was best. It took a lot of hiking."

"Holy smokes," laughed Ralph. "Back when I was locating trail, I lived out of a frying pan. I made my own bannock. That's the same as biscuit dough only you put it in a fry pan. You mix it up, so much baking powder and salt and flour, and you make it just like biscuit dough so it'll stay when you tip the pan up to catch the heat from the fire."

Was he lonesome? "No," he said. "You had to be so you wouldn't get lonesome. You'd go off by yourself [locating trails] and when night came, you'd bed down and go to sleep. I just came by it naturally. Some others got so homesick they had to leave."

SEARCHING FOR STORIES is analogous to prospecting for gold. There was one memorable spring morning when I managed to combine the two. I took Glee Davis (1885–1982) out to the North Cascades Mountains both to learn about the "stampeders" who'd hacked a crude trail up the river and to find some gold of my own. Ninety-five-year-old Glee and I rocked our pans in the Skagit's icy water until our fingers ached. I was confident that his knowledge and my strength would combine to make us rich.

Glee inundated his foot-wide, mud-filled pan until clear water climbed its slanted sides. He renewed his steady, horizontal shaking to sort out any gold from dross. The gravel varied from pebbles to coarse grit to fine, suspended silt. My teacher's gnarled hands splashed the half-sunk pan left and right, back and forth. The stony soil protested noisily against the metal as he swirled the muddy

mix. What surprised me was that Glee's rhythm was so practiced that he was less fatigued than I was as we bent to our labor.

Glee Davis was not an impressive man by today's materialistic standards. He never did much except pack horses on the Upper Skagit, pan a little gold, raise a family, and live a very long time. But that was enough for me. I used to spend hour after hour at his house in Sedro-Woolley listening to his tales of the miners and eccentrics who worked the wild, free headwaters of the Skagit River. Glee's stories took me back to 1893 when he homesteaded with his beloved mother Lucinda on Cascade Creek. Later in the 1890s, he helped her to operate a roadhouse on an Upper Skagit gravel bar (today located beneath Diablo Lake).

Glee earned his living until the early 1920s by mule-freighting supplies in to the Upper Skagit River's mines. As he neared the century mark, only his wheezy lungs showed any signs of giving out. Unlike many people both young and old, he was not desperate to cling to this life. After one bad bout with his worn-out lungs he told me, "I wasn't very much worried. I thought, if this is the end, well, let it be." Nevertheless, he was soon working again in his big garden. I admired that spirit and hoped that when the time came, I, too, would be as philosophical about letting go.

Before we began our prospecting trip, Glee had chided me because my new pan was greasy. "Well," he chuckled, "we'll have to smoke that up over a campfire."

"What?" I asked in horror. "Smoke it up!"

"Don't you see that grease on there? They come like that to keep 'em from rusting. We'd always heat a new one over a fire to get down to the metal. Otherwise, the grease traps the gold dust."

I suddenly realized that I had a lot to learn about prospecting—even if all I wanted was just one big nugget. In fact, I had to become serious about mining or lose the six dollars invested in my gold pan. So I spent five dollars more on a reproduction of a Yukon gold rush guide called *Placer Mining: A Hand-Book for Klondike & Other Miners and Prospectors*. But I figured that even at a conservative price per ounce I could soon earn back this eleven dollar outlay.

My *Hand-Book* was full of quaint advice on dissolving citric acid in water "to make lemonade in case of scurvy" and on keeping one's fur clothes in good repair since "one slit may cause untold agony during a march in a heavy storm." I read enthusiastically about hydraulic mining with elaborate flumes and pipes; thawing frozen pay dirt with charcoal fires; and separating gold from dross with puddling boxes, bateas, rockers, Toms, and sluices. Finally, I found a description of how to use a gold pan "pressed from a single sheet of Russia iron." Nothing to it, I thought.

"You can't make any money panning unless it's very rich," Glee warned. He fingered the gravel. "We probably won't find anything," he said. "Hardly anyone did and they went all over this stream. Any colors have been ground into flour."

"Am I doing this right?" I asked, still hoping for at least a small nugget.

"You don't have to bury it quite so deep. Just so the gravel is covered. Anything weighty like gold will descend in the pan. As you shake it, the lighter rocks will be on top. Take them off but be careful not to throw away pieces of gold."

I stared intently at the muck in my pan.

"Shake it a little harder."

"Did you ever find anything?" I asked.

"I never found any nuggets of any size. Oh, at the old price of seventeen dollars I'd find something worth twenty-five or thirty-five cents." He pointed at my pan. "Keep pouring that dirt off."

"Seventeen dollars an ounce!" I cried.

"Yes, that was the price as far back as I can remember."

Glee's black, antique pan fascinated me and I asked him about it. "When we first went up as far as Ruby Creek in 1898," he said, "prospectors were all over. You'd have a time finding room for a claim. That year I got this pan from some miners who were preparing to go out."

My arms and back were getting tired. "I didn't realize panning involved so much shaking," I said wearily.

"It's tedious," admitted Glee, "but if you find richer dirt, you can pan a little faster. If you could be where City Light flooded, it's very rich there. Well, there's pretty close to four hundred feet of water on top of it now."

"I think this would be a hard way to make a living," I said, resting a moment.

"Yes, it is and those old prospectors had a pretty rough life. But they were happy. Always thinking they were gonna strike it rich."

"I wonder if there's a certain kind of person who becomes obsessed with searching for gold?" I asked.

"Why, you will," laughed Glee, "if you find some. It won't take you more than a day or so and you'll be saying, 'I want to try that strike up there.'"

"Sure, if I find something," I grinned, knowing he was right. "But what about the people who waste their whole lives at it?"

"Some will do that, but usually they don't have families. They just go out, live by themselves, and prospect."

"Well," he continued, looking at my pan, "you're doing a good job panning that gray mud off. In this country, black sand is an indicator of possible gold. You want to be very careful when the black sand is getting all up right at the head of the bar." He pointed to the higher side of his pan, away from him. "See it getting black there."

"Why is the top of the pan called the head of the bar?" I asked.

"Like a gravel bar, you know. Here's the stream coming through and there's a little bar in the pan with a head and a tail. You'll find the gold right at the head of that bar in with the black sand."

"Yes, I can definitely see the black sand," I said excitedly. "What do we do now?"

"Just shake it on down. Save your black sand even if you think there's no gold in it 'cause there is gold there. You can dry it out, run a magnet through it, and scrape it off into a box."

I was very disappointed by the end of the day that we had accumulated only a few grains of black sand—and no gold. "Maybe panning is not for me?" I sighed.

I ALWAYS LIKE to visit Marblemount, Washington, the former outfitting center for the Upper Skagit River's miners, dam builders, and trappers. Today's respectable tourist businesses are a far cry from old Marblemount's saloons and sporting houses. And it was the original, riproarin', wide-open settlement that I wanted to hear about from storekeeper Otto Peterson (1896–1986).

Despite being "buggered up" with arthritis, Otto regaled me with nonstop stories of making money on everything from undeveloped land to unaged whiskey. In 1922 he had been an automobile salesman on the coast when he bought a cheap house and store in Marblemount, on the condition, enforced by his wife, that he would sell the properties in six months at most. But instead he had persuaded her to move to this last outpost up the Skagit River, a place so backward that its prime modes of transport were dugout canoes and pack strings. Wife or no wife, the business opportunities were too good to resist, he said. "I owned the *only* store here," he told me gleefully.

Part of his fun involved the fistfights that often broke out at his second-floor dance hall. "There was no fighting allowed up there and they knew it," he said. "If they started anything, the two men were grabbed so damn fast they didn't know what happened and taken outside. The rest of the people brought gas lanterns and let the boys fight in the street. No gloves. No protection. Just go right in there and try to kill each other. Every once in a while there'd be a man in the circle whose friend was getting the worst of it and he'd start to dive in there to help. Somebody would knock him on his butt so fast he wouldn't know what happened. It was a fair fight. Some of 'em would need a few stitches but nothing they couldn't recover from. You never saw a prize fight as good as some of the fights we had!"

"Your store must have been quite a social center," I gulped.

"It was the only store for miles and miles. And all these miners, loggers, dam builders, and prospectors. All this progress! They had to have everything." And everything is what Otto sold. He was literally as well as figuratively the ultimate horse trader. "People used to bring herds of horses to sell," he said, "because their country east of the mountains was overrun with horses. They'd bring 'em to this ranch across the river and pretty soon they couldn't sell any more. So I'd give 'em a dollar a head for what was left and take the men and their families to the train at Rockport. They'd go home on the train. I peddled their horses."

"That sounds like a good deal," I said.

"It was *all right*," he laughed craftily. "I sold one of those horses for a hundred and twenty dollars as soon as I got home from taking the people to the train."

"Oh, I had everything at the store," he continued. "You could come in and buy dry goods by the yard. You could buy silk hose, shoes, clothing. You could buy horse feed, dynamite, anything from a bag of peanuts to a ton of sugar."

"A ton of sugar?" I laughed. "Oh, for moonshine. I guess someone was selling moonshine here." (I soon learned that a large part of Otto's success stemmed from Washington's having become a "dry" state in 1914.)

"Who wasn't?" said Otto. "Well, I've sold many a barrel of whiskey. It cost a dollar and a half to make a gallon. I'd buy it for six dollars a gallon and sell it in the dance hall for two dollars a short pint, ten pints to the gallon."

"That's a *real* short pint!" I protested.

"No," said Otto defensively, "that's the way we used to sell it. Two dollars a short pint in a little flat bottle. We were all bootleggers. You could buy whiskey from me or Sadie or Ma Wright or the packer. We all had a little on hand. There were people around Marblemount who made huge fortunes and retired on moonshine."

Otto told me a story about two professional moonshiners who paid him cash for complete supplies for a very elaborate still. They bragged about how they were going to get rich but the first morning before they had even made a run the sheriff "smashed their still to hell." As Otto said, "They'd put all their money into the still and sugar and meal, and when the sheriff got through with it, all they could do was sell it for scrap copper. If it had been my still, I don't think the sheriff would have knocked it over. I was well thought of in the sheriff's department."

In fact, because Otto was a friend of the sheriff he managed to get one of the moonshiners out of jail. As a reward the poor fellow gave him a deed to his last bit of property, forty good acres near Marblemount. "I got it clear title," laughed Otto proudly.

As a storekeeper, Otto never distilled moonshine himself except for one memorable batch. He explained that two men had used dugout canoes to set up large vats and a big still across the river—inaccessible in that roadless country since the nearest bridge was miles downstream. He said, "Well, they came to town with some of the brew. It was good drinking stuff even before you ran it through the still. Like a beer but with a much higher proof. Anyway, they were foolin' around town and here come this sudden storm and the river just went wild. Flood stage. Trees and logs: all kinds of drift coming down. And here their brew was ready to run and they didn't dare to cross the river. So they were going to lose the whole batch."

"So what happened?" I asked.

"Well, they was cryin' because they had hundreds of dollars invested. They offered me half the whiskey if I'd go and run it. Their brand new ten-gallon kegs were over there and it was all ready to go.

"I knew a young chap, another horse's ass about my age, whose dad was a moonshiner so he'd worked around stills. I never had. We talked this over and he said he'd cross with me in a dugout canoe. He was a damned good canoeman and I wasn't too bad. So we went over and fired up the still and saved the batch. They gave us half the whiskey. So we made a few hundred dollars there in two days!"

ONCE LONG AGO at the coastal village of La Push, I needed a ride across the Quillayute River to continue my hike up the Wilderness Coast. Luckily I struck up a conversation with a Native American boatbuilder at his waterfront home.

I passed a derelict dugout canoe where it rested in a jumble of boats, bikes, debris, and weeds. Entering an open workshop, I shook a hand greasy from outboard motor parts. Thomas "Ribs" Penn (1930–1994) wore a logger shirt, blue jeans, Seahawks cap, and a button, "Rebel And Proud Of It." A heavy smoker despite a recent heart attack, he told me that as a child he'd been so scrawny that people had called him Ribs. I replied, stating the obvious, that I was still skinny. He regarded me as if he were sizing up a canoe tree for straightness. "You're okay," he said, "but you'll put on weight just like I did."

Ribs offered to take me upriver for a little joyride after he got his motor fixed. In the chaos of his workshop, everything was near at hand but arranged according to no visible system; the work went slowly. When at last he muscled the heavy motor onto the sloping stern of his everyday boat, he said that he was happiest when he was building canoes and fishing for salmon. Of course, I wanted to hear about both.

I readily accepted Ribs's invitation to show me his beloved river. I loaded my pack and myself into the *L'il Dewey* and sat back to enjoy the ride as the weathered but graceful dugout pulled away from the empty anchorages. Amidships, leaning against a thwart, there was nothing between me and the river's deep channel but an inch of cedar. The boat's gray paint was so badly chipped that earlier hues peeked through.

"If everything goes good, it might take a month to build one," said Ribs. "The most difficult part is shaping the front and back so that they match. You get scared someone will say, 'Hey, look at that guy; he cut too much out.'" For the umpteenth time Ribs emphasized the pride he and the few remaining canoe builders took in their art of axe, chainsaw, and adze.

We saw a half dozen Indians checking their stationary nets as we motored slowly a few miles up the river. Lines of white floats marked the nylon gillnets that reached into the alder-bordered river from anchor points ashore. When salmon or steelhead swam upstream, they became enmeshed—and easy spoils for the net owner unless a 50- to 60-pound king salmon tore through the net or voracious seals stole the catch.

We stopped to say hello to two of Ribs's many friends. The man and his young son were lifting their net by hand, bit by bit into their skiff. They beat the nylon mesh with sticks to free it of river-borne debris, then dumped the occasional king or silver into their boat. The salmon were beautiful specimens of everything a fish should be. After four mysterious years at sea, they were plump and shiny and averaged 10 to 30 pounds.

Being out on the water released something in the normally taciturn Ribs. He talked animatedly about what it had been like to net fish from a canoe with his father. "We always went up the river after a three or four day freshet," he said, "when the river was high. Father's dugout canoes for fishing were a lot bigger than today's. He'd leave before daybreak. Get back at dark. And go out again immediately. Days and nights. Fish never waited for no one. But I am afraid that net fishing out of a canoe is now a lost art because there are so few days when we're allowed to fish."

Sometimes our upstream progress through the Quillayute's braids and sloughs was slowed almost to a halt by shallows. Then Ribs pulled up the motor and resorted to his triangular, homemade paddle to move us into deeper currents. He seemed to know every twist and turn of this high-volume torrent. Ribs said that he never became tired of the river, that he always found something to love in her wildness.

As we sat floating with the current, I asked how he'd happened to build his first canoe. "Learning canoe building from my grandfather, Esau Penn, was one of the best things that ever happened to me," he said. "The way he chopped on a canoe! When he first started to work on one, he could chop either right- or left-handed. I was embarrassed to ask what he was going to do next so I just watched. The only measurement he ever made was from one end of the heart to the other. The width and angles were all in his mind.

"I tried to use a ruler one time but I chucked that aside and just went by sight. You can stand at the end and pretty well tell how you want it. It takes skill and a lot of luck. I seem to know when to quit chopping. You learn from your mistakes. You learn easier ways for each step.

"The eagerness of wanting to use the canoe will make you maybe make a mistake. Especially toward the end. And the log alone might cost five thousand dollars from a mill. So I get my mind off it. I walk down to the water. I talk to the grass. Anything."

I was surprised that although Ribs insisted vehemently on the value of his traditions, he said that non-Indians were more appreciative of them. He said that he was unable to persuade local youths to take up the canoe-making challenge. It was obvious that Ribs derived pleasure not only from building canoes but also from handling them out on the river. It was a treat to see him maneuver among the currents, sand bars, and vegetation. I felt that in his own way he was a local hero. Using simple materials and tools, he had created a legacy for others to treasure.

Novices sometimes begin to build more dugout canoes than they can finish. The incomplete failures that are left to lie in the woods are called "bush canoes." It was obvious to me that Ribs Penn was no bush canoe. Metaphorically he was still all that a dugout should be: functional and beautiful. Despite the fact that his cedar was cracked, patched, and in need of paint, his two-foot-high gunwales were sturdy, and his carved prow was still ready to slice through waves. Ribs Penn was a classic.

Murder Mystery at the Old Mine

*We'd send one man in with a thousand or fifteen hundred
head right up close to Chopaka Lake to ride and put out
salt. Pretty soon we'd move 'em back a little further, and
then we'd move 'em clean back to Snowshoe Camp and
all through there. Then clean over to Horseshoe Basin. Of
course, we'd go in every once in awhile to see how they was.
[Near the end of the season] when it come time to take the
beef out, we'd go back in there and gather 'em. Later in the
fall, we'd gather the cows after the first snow. I've rode back
in there in regular old blizzards. God, it was cold as the
dickens.*

Paul Louden, *River Pigs and Cayuses*, 1984

MILES FROM ANYWHERE, the Pasayten Wilderness is ironically
where I have met some of the Pacific Northwest Trail's most
sociable folks. There was even a night at the old Tungsten Mine
when some of us tried to solve a murder mystery.

Long a mecca for backcountry conviviality, the mine's cabin,
corrals, cook house, and ruined workings were a legacy from Paul
Louden (1891–1982). I loved that man though we had next to
nothing in common. His education had begun in the saddle at age
twelve. Unschooled, he followed his pioneer father into ranching.
He was also a butcher, whiskey runner, rodeo star, and even mayor
of Oroville, Washington. "We got a good education for what we
wanted," he once told me, "which was to be cattlemen." And,
related to this chapter's story, during World War I he had freighted
mining supplies to a claim well west of the Pasayten's Horseshoe
Basin.

I interviewed Paul for my 1984 oral history *River Pigs and
Cayuses*. Thereafter, each time I hiked past the Tungsten Mine I
enjoyed seeing his metal bathtub. He'd packed it in from a distant

trailhead atop a donkey named Jack. I remember one particular August 13 when I found that four Oroville horsemen had moved the heavy antique out of the cook house to use as a horse trough. Each man had known Paul, and our reminiscences led to a jolly repartee of news and gossip. I was fascinated by the old boys' blending of births, deaths, jobs, illnesses, weddings, affairs, promotions, binges, and kin into a kind of oral news blog. The old-timers included an Oroville city councilman, a wilderness drover, and the brother of a cattleman whom I'd met eleven years earlier. I already knew the youngest man, fortyish Bob Neal, a body shop owner and tow truck driver.

Horsemen tend to fill their panniers with heavy goodies that amaze ounce-conscious backpackers. One man invited me to polish off a can of pears and a bag of cookies. Always hungry, I did not need to be asked twice. Later the boys passed around a bottle. The stove burned hot, and the lantern cast shadows on log walls where generations of backcountry travelers had left their spoor. I walked around the room reading the prosaic, written-on-wood messages in the light of my headlamp.

> *Bill Franke and Jack Abrams passed through here June 18, 1934 to Cathedral Lakes. Returned June 21, 1934. Fishing was excellent.*

Just when I was ready to turn in for the night, someone mentioned an inscription about the mysterious disappearance of a trapper. Bob Neal found the words for me.

> *January 18, 1931. Snow level with roof of this cabin. Temperature 6 degrees above C. No sign of Arnold. Pulling out tomorrow. James C. Thornton*

January 1931 was no ordinary time in the Pasayten. Between 1917 and 1930, drought-enhanced fires had burned hundreds of thousands of acres. And now a man was lost in that desolate country.

I located a further description by someone else:

Arnold found on Horseshoe near mouth.
Hung by neck.
June 15, 1935.   C. H. J.

The hiss of the white gas lantern seemed more sinister as the Oroville horsemen discussed how Arnold might have died. Popular opinion held that the trapper had somehow broken a leg. Rather than starve to death, he had hanged himself.

Or was it murder? My new friends seemed to think so. Bob Neal thought that a renegade fur trapper from Winthrop had killed Arnold, hung him up, and then sold his furs. When someone later tried to sell those pelts, the fur merchant had notified the sheriff, who then tracked the seller into the mountains without success.

I wished that our mutual friend, Paul Louden, had been with us to share our palaver. With Paul's frontier passion for visiting and talking, I can only imagine the fantastical elements he would have added to the tale of the dead trapper and the missing furs.

It is shortsighted to think of wilderness solely in terms of solitude. During that Tungsten Mine visit I observed that the tunnels had long ago collapsed, leaving treacherous depressions near the dilapidated refining works. The site was littered with pipes, wheels, gears, grates, fireboxes, rails, shovels, ore carts, iron and steel of every shape. An old gravity mill deteriorated in peace as rusting, freezing, thawing, and cracking worked their will. Already fireweed, that harbinger of future fruitfulness, grew on the sand, gravel, and talus.

That mine's few buildings are Pasayten treasures more valuable than any ore that was ever found. There is a temptation to understand wilderness only in the *absence* of humans. I prefer a more complete view that treasures the backcountry's legends and tales. Such stories sit lightly on the land and add immeasurably to our enjoyment.

I wish I could tell trapper Arnold that he did not die in vain. His story will long continue to enthrall travelers to that splendid country, hard up on the border, far from anywhere.

Along the PNT: The Okanogan

If you know your West at all, you know its Western Yellow Pine ... Its dry and spacious groves invite you to camp among them ... No conifers are finer than these for a walk beneath their boughs.

Donald Cullross Peatie
A Natural History of North American Trees, 2007

REPUBLIC, WASHINGTON, occupied rolling hills typical of the eastern Okanogan's highlands. I hauled my sorry self into town on the kind of afternoon when asphalt gloms onto boots like chewing gum. After a 20-mile road slog, I gratefully settled into a window seat in a cool restaurant with a good view of listless folk trudging to the post office, Forest Service, credit union, and barber shop. A baby bawled in her stroller, but the mother was too listless to care.

Torpidly sipping a drink, I was overcome by a wonderful daydream in which everyone shared my passion for the trail. I dreamed that Republic's good citizens embraced backpacking. Merchants closed up shop. Salesmen ceased their peddling. Hospital patients found cures on the trail. County commissioners decreed, "A pack on every back."

Clearly I had been out in the sun too long.

But the funny thing was that Republic had, about a century before, fallen prey to an equally unlikely fantasy: gold. The reality was that the town's sun-scorched grasslands and fir/pine forests had been transformed in 1896 as a gold mining camp named Eureka. Then in 1898, Congress at the behest of local promoters had opened the nearby South Half of the Colville Indian Reservation to fortune hunters. An early-twentieth-century history of the area tells the story:

There was the greatest commotion possible in every quarter ... By two o'clock AM, just as gray dawn was creeping over the eastern hills, at least sixty men had mounted and departed southward, leaving a trail of dust behind them. Youth and old age were in the race; prospector and novice were pushing forward. All night the hegira continued. The sound of horses' feet and the loud voices of the riders kept many drowsy people awake, and curiosity brought not a few to the street and a realizing sense that something unusual was in the air. Old "gin pigs," asleep in chairs, staggered up and feebly attempted to gain some idea of the situation; night hawks, those birds of prey, were around and got many a dram from departing citizens. All day Friday the exodus continued.

My recurring fantasy always portrays a future in which a substantial number of people of all ages will be drawn to hiking. Gold will not be their imagined reward (unless they manufacture some sort of irresistible, new ultralight equipment). Yes, indeed, this daydream is not as farfetched as it may seem. And the Okanogan has many of the riches that can make it come true.

ONE EVENING the vast, high steppe spread to the horizon from my evening perch on Mount Bonaparte's 7258-foot summit. As night fell, the Kettle Range shouldered up the eastern sky. Republic's rough hills and buttes were echoed farther west by more valleys, draws, and clearcuts all the way to the outlier mountains of the Pasayten Wilderness. From my aerie, the massive cliffs of the PNT's Chopaka Mountain route looked virtually impassable. I fell asleep dreaming of those distant hints of the wildlands to come.

Awaking at midnight in the summit's twinkling firmament, I scanned the dark Okanogan highlands for ranch lights, which showed where people slept beneath the white spine of the Milky Way. Backpacking, I thought, was not just about putting one foot in front of the other. It was an accumulation of small details and daily routines, of unexpected trials and joys, and of solitary insights and shared moments. Like the galaxy above my head, it was both real and transcendent.

It took me 1½ days to walk from Mt. Bonaparte to Oroville, another former gold camp. Along the way, I dropped from 7258 feet elevation to only 926 feet, and saw enough rattlers and grasshoppers to believe the official statistic about August rainfall averaging just over half an inch. Creosote brush's thick, glossy leaves and deep taproots reminded me that each microclimate had its own adaptation to aridity. Yellow stonecrop lined ledges of crumbling, stained basalt. Stiff deer tufts hung on thorns and sagebrush. An impossibly blue sky capped the bluffs, buttes, and badlands.

Ponderosa pines, the dominant trees of this parched country, looked as if the russet scales of their scarred trunks had withstood five hundred years of fires. The largest grew in delightful park-like settings because each tree's extensive root system needs a lot of space from which to collect the ground's scarce moisture. The trees' airy grace was so delicate that I often stopped just to watch the interplay of springy boughs, brilliant light, and long needles. Naturalist John Muir had felt my same affection for ponderosas when he wrote, "Of all the pines this one gives forth the finest music to the winds."

THE WESTMOST part of the Okanogan National Forest offers some of the finest hiking that I have ever seen. From Horseshoe Basin west, the parklands with their lodgepole pine, Engelman spruce, and sub-alpine fir eventually give way to open ridges and deep, forested valleys. Major 6000- to 8000-foot peaks add to the fun.

I first fell under this country's spell in 1970. I remember my delight in arcing west, up out of the Methow Valley, to Apex Pass. Below to my left, two golden eagles soared thermals to search for small game. Their brown airfoils made me feel very earthbound.

As the sun strengthened its grip on the morning, I peeled off layers of clothing. On the way to Cathedral Pass, trail dust coated my legs as I walked through a scraggly forest of young lodgepole pines. The landscape was peppered with silvery old snags, as if a giant porcupine had filled the land with quills. Monochrome weathered ridges and tumbled granite boulders were brightened by the intense yellows of mountain buttercups and by the whites and purples of yarrows and gentians. It all came together in my mind as a Picasso dinosaur. The great tower of Cathedral Peak was a cubist painting of Manhattan skyscrapers—gray overall but darker where slabs had broken off. Where a trail crew had dynamited the granite, the fresh surface glowed brilliantly in the sun.

A great spectacle of Nature greeted me at windy Cathedral Pass. Back the way I had come were the Chewack Valley's fire-killed snags and its nearby ring of unscathed larches. Beside me to either side were gleaming patches of last season's snow. Above to my right was the immensity of Cathedral Peak, now less like a painting than a fluid sculpture in stone. Ahead were the wooded, rocky basins of the Cathedral Lakes country. I wrote in my journal, "I have been out in incredibly beautiful country for two months but today's beauty feels like an almost physical balm."

As I continued my walk west, the long ridge and mountain views were to become even more spectacular. Nearing the crest of the Cascades this scenic intensity increased as valleys became deeper, steeper, and narrower. The granitic gneisses of the North Cascades form the most awesome alpine complex in the Lower Forty-eight. There are 127 high lakes, over three hundred glaciers, countless snowfields, and untold numbers of rivulets, creeks, and rivers. In the midst of such splendor, I chose my campsites for the maximum possible overdose of scenery.

The aptly named Devil's Dome was such a place—a rocky, wind-blasted, inhospitable, magnificent throne in the sky. Across the awesome chasm of Devil's Creek, glacier-clad Jack Mountain rose 7500 feet from nearby Ross Lake. To enjoy the spectacle I set up my tent in the lee of some sub-alpine firs below Devil's Dome's exposed summit. The scenery was so rich in every direction that I sat until well after sunset taking in all the peaks, angles, drops, and voids. Glacier-bedecked Jack Mountain dominated the south. Westward were the Pickets. Startlingly white Mount Baker poked a hole in the sunset horizon. But as mountain-sized shadows lengthened across the North Cascades, my gaze was more and more drawn to a Valhalla-like fortress of a peak to the north. No name could have done justice to that crenulated vision of fairytale empire. The dark blue of Hozomeen's citadel deepened into a pure black keep, impregnable, inviolate like the Cascades themselves.

This was an evening when the sky's structures matched in majesty those of the land. Anvil-shaped thunderheads rose in muscular, white billows to stratospheric heights. A line of boiling confections walled off the eastern sky. Scattershot blasts of light burst up and down the front like a cannonade.

In the nineteenth century, men valued the backcountry for its gold. But the best moments of my life have been times such as that evening on Devil's Dome when I measured my wealth in sunsets and satisfaction. Happy me: walking was and is my path to riches.

Trail Magic

Pollen enough to choke, heat enough to cook with, humidity enough to boil. Dueling mutant rats & giant blacksnakes. Weird-ass day from hell. But great trail magic (twice) and good laughter in the evening made all well. Go figure.
"Bear Paw," Appalachian Trail thru-hiker
Dick's Dome Shelter, June 1, 1999

TRAIL MAGIC is a relatively new phrase to describe serendipitous good fortune while hiking. Examples include those surprise moments when we receive a gift from a stranger or from Nature. For instance, I was once overwhelmed with joy when someone caught up to me with the diary that I had left behind in a particularly remote part of the Sierra. Trail magic also took the form of an all-I-could-eat meal after I, ill and starving, bailed out from the high Sierra down the trailless South Fork of the Kings River.

There should always be an element of wonder about trail magic. "Wow, I don't believe this!" says a little voice in my head. A spoilsport might chalk up such events to coincidence or sheer randomness. But I remember that my mentor Paris Walters, a great believer in *synchronicity*, always relished telling me about his latest inexplicable experience. His trail magic was never the prosaic, "Hey guys, I found some unopened beers in the creek." Similarly, my favorite examples usually concern feelings. Best of all are the occasions when I can step out of my solitary trail life to find that I have become part of a community.

DURING THE 1970s, northeast Washington's rural counterculture, known locally as Hill People, formed communes, planted organic gardens, raised goats, and read *Mother Earth News*. In 1979 when I attended their Barter Fair in a forest-ringed pasture near Ione, Washington, I found the expected tie-dye clothes, Old Testament beards, Sioux tepees, bare breasts, smoky fires, and colorful busses. Luckily I also discovered one of the event's organizers. No Name was a slightly built, New York refugee who had earlier run afoul of the Forest Service for having illegally grazed his goats on public land. He'd tried unsuccessfully to beat that rap by arguing that his animals were merely traveling companions, not conventional livestock. Curiously enough, his louche pets had partially inspired the Barter Fair. As he rhythmically squeezed goat teats, he told me that he and others wanted to trade their surplus milk and cheese in order to obtain the additional food that their families needed. He believed that the Barter Fair was not just a social networking phenomenon but also a communitarian economic model. But he thought that he could live a subsistence lifestyle if he were able to trade his surplus for staples at a harvest fair.

The Barter Fair was evidently an exercise in frugality and fellowship, two qualities dear to my heart. I wanted to participate, but I had nothing to trade. That changed dramatically when I noticed a crumbling log cabin surrounded by frost-whitened weeds. After I accidentally trampled some of them, the air filled with a rich, familiar scent. Eureka! I rolled one of the gelid, four-sided stems in my fingers to release its powerful fragrance. Thanks to the cabin's long-ago owner, I now had something to barter. In twenty minutes I gathered enough mint to fill a large duffel bag.

I had never before hawked anything except my dream of the Pacific Northwest Trail. A salesman I was not. But now, inspired by No Name, I hauled my wares toward the chapati vendors, robed gurus, astrological seers, and loose dogs. Unsure how to begin, I let lust be my guide, and chatted up a shapely, scantily clad young woman who was trying to unload her commune's dusty books. She readily exchanged *The Complete Plays Of Aristophanes* for a few sprigs of mint. I was certain that the master of Greek comedy would have approved my pumping her for information about my weeds' many benefits. I learned that, whether as an infusion or as a seasoning, mint was a tasty cure-all for a wide range of medical complaints.

Even when I wasn't trying, the stuff sold itself. With little effort and much fun my hoard soon included four golden delicious apples; a large watermelon; a three-pound loaf of whole wheat bread; a two-pound loaf of Cornell bread; four tomatoes; a ceramic pumpkin (created by Satya, owner of the fair site); a large jar of kosher pickles; two jars of plum jam (of which one was later traded for three bars of homemade soap in mint, orange, and lavender scents); two jars of blackberry jam (of which one was traded for an antique milk bottle); a bunch of fresh sage; a cantaloupe; a squash (type unknown); two tacos (lunch); a jar of honey; two glasses of pear juice; a jar of pitted cherries; and a delicious dinner cooked over a campfire in a teepee. Through bartering I met friendly, optimistic people who shared No Name's dream of a rural, alternative society.

That evening one of my best trades earned me a delicious fire-pit-cooked meal in one of the dozens of tepees. Glowing coals were my only light as I tried to sate both my hunger and my curiosity. The former was easy, but I kept wondering as I eavesdropped on people's conversations if they had any clue about preparing for winter or for the education of their children. I marveled at the Hill People's faith in astrology and other daft fads. Yet listening to the animated talk around me, I had a sudden sense of my own separation from family and friends. Most days, for years on end, I was perfectly happy to live a hiking lifestyle focused on what was over the next horizon. I was doing exactly what interested me. But there were sometimes moments when the rootedness of other people reminded me that perhaps my choices were not as emotionally cost-free as I habitually thought. At the Barter Fair I could not help but notice that though many of its nomads and squatters lived in dirt-floor wickiups, they were far more settled than I was.

After dinner, when I stepped outside into the cold air, the full moon had just risen, yellow and welcoming. I stood quietly amid the aboriginal geometry of tepees that beckoned hypnotically like a scene from prehistory. Smoke rose from distant campfires as a chorus of *OMs* greeted the moon.

Somewhere in the distance a woman began to sing a beautiful lullaby. I walked toward the sound until I came to a dark Mongolian yurt. Just as the song ended, I pulled aside the canvas flap door and peeked into the squat, round, shelter. Among the dozen people who welcomed me to their song circle, I recognized some of No Name's friends.

I was too mesmerized by the memory of that lyrical voice to concentrate on the how-to talk of sweat lodges and goat pens. I barely noticed the infants and toddlers who slept, tucked out of the way among the food containers and wooden bowls. Above me, the conical roof narrowed to a vent hole where smoke danced in a blue shaft of moonlight.

The yurt's owners were ensconced on a dais of pillows. Sandra, whose voice had so intrigued me, was a lovely woman about my own age. Her shoulder-length chestnut hair was straight except for one braid. When we met, she encompassed me in her beautiful smile and spoke as if she had known me forever. She said that she'd had to go through "a lot of dying" to shed her conservative Southern ways to open up to people. Her "old man," William (who literally looked a generation older), had played a large part, she said, in helping her. So had her two children, including a baby by William.

Sandra and William had met at the first Barter Fair. "He came dancing up to me," she beamed, "dressed only in a loincloth, this strange, *sadhu*-looking man. I'd never seen anybody like that before!" Sandra had then only recently come out from Georgia, but before long she and William were a Barter Fair family, trading their leatherwork, and living in a squatter's shelter they built on state land.

Sandra's mother, a Great Depression escapee to the suburbs, could not understand why her daughter had chosen such a barefoot, penurious lifestyle. The answer, Sandra said, was that friends supplied her with exactly the warmth that her materialistic mother was incapable of giving.

Longhaired William looked every inch the guru, with kindly eyes that seemed to understand the world's vanity and folly. Soon he captivated us all with the story of two Hindu deities who had the power to reveal the number of rebirths that people must endure before being absorbed into the One. When the two immortals encountered a group of monks, a self-centered fellow (who was very proud of his fastidious *asanas*) asked to know the future. That man complained bitterly when the deities told him that his torment in the cycle of rebirth would continue for a thousand lifetimes. After disclosing the other men's fates, it was time for the two visitors to leave. Just then a kind-hearted, humble drunkard awoke after sleeping off some wine. When he learned of his sanctimonious brother's thousand remaining lifetimes, he exclaimed with joy, "After that he will be free! *How lucky*!"

The deities heard him and invited the good fellow to dance. The three then stepped round and round, faster and faster, until they spun so quickly that they became a flame, a twinkling fire that absorbed the humble monk into the heavens. In an instant his chain of rebirth was broken.

After William's story, everyone sang a sentimental song for No Name and his pregnant mate Silver Moon, who had just entered the yurt with their child Raspberry. That little family of three glowed at the center of a circle of affection that to my great pleasure included me.

To be part of a loving community is the best trail magic of all.

Along the PNT: Roll On, Columbia, Roll On

Becoming a trail angel was an excellent way to meet
fascinating types of people that I wouldn't ordinarily have
encountered. The thru-hikers always had great stories to tell,
and they were Nature people who helped me to see things
here in Northport from a different perspective.
Ollie Mae Wilson, PNT trail angel from 1983 to 2009

LONG AGO, in 1972, at the end of an arduous day of exploration high in the forests east of the Columbia River, I noticed the name Lind Ranch on my map, and I began to dream of baked treats and warm hospitality. Exhausted from slogging through a confusing maze of muddy logging roads, I had a pie craving to end all such fantasies.

However, no baker welcomed me onto the Lind Ranch's rainswept meadows. Dark forms of log ruins revealed that the place had been abandoned. Beneath the barn's steep-pitched roof, Farmer Lind's last cutting of hay was compressed by time and tunneled by mice. I spread out my sleeping bag on his musty bedding and settled in for a long night. Acutely regretting my lack of hot pie and warm conversation, I was in a pensive mood as the squall swept darkly across the meadow and the encircling forest.

Wherever I go on the PNT I am alert for echoes of the past. Part of the pleasure of hiking is to know that I am in the company of homesteaders, gold miners, trail locators, boundary mappers, mule skinners, and nomadic Natives. A man on foot has a lot of time to ponder those who have gone before him, but what he is really doing is creating his own narrative that he can reflect upon and enjoy later.

Wondering about rancher Lind, I peered from his barn at a tufted-eared silhouette high in a fir tree. After its wild hoots punctuated the darkness, the great horned owl swooped to the edge of the

meadow to hunt chipmunks, voles, and ground squirrels. A young buck slipped cautiously into the clearing.

The sound of rain on the meadow was as soft as the dim light itself. Though the farm was a perfect refuge for owls and dreamers, I wondered why the owner had built in such an inhospitable spot. The hand-crafted look of Lind's homestead was not the work of a transient or a speculator. His log farmhouse, barn, and outbuildings were well built and would still have been sound if they had been maintained.

I was certain that the ranch must have been doomed financially from the beginning—the site was too high, too exposed, too unproductive even in the best years. I felt that the monetary prospects could not have been what tied Lind to the long winters, spring rains, and wild beauty.

ELEVEN YEARS LATER, snow, rain, sun, and wind had completed the collapse of the hay-filled barn where I had weathered that storm. All that was left was a jumble of nettles and rotting poles. But the greatest change was not in the ruins themselves but in my understanding of what I saw. A local friend had informed me that what I'd thought was a failed ranch was merely a high summer pasture. I learned that, yes, Lind was a solitary old cuss but nothing like the hermit I had imagined.

I was unable to sleep in his barn again to catch up on the owl news that the broader world had ignored. And I failed to thank Herman Lind for that night in the straw and for the gentle sound of meadow rain that still murmured to me across the years.

"ROLL ON, COLUMBIA, Roll on," sang Woody Guthrie, troubadour of two dozen Bonneville Power Administration tunes in the 1930s. "Your power is turning our darkness to dawn, So roll on, Columbia, roll on."

Northport, Washington, is an important town on the PNT because of its Columbia River crossing near the tail end of Franklin

D. Roosevelt Lake. When I walked through three decades ago, the sun-blasted hills west of the river were so hot that I kept to whichever side of the road had even the slightest hint of shade. Even a skinny dip beneath a highway bridge brought only temporary relief. Though there were plenty of people out there with me, there was no one to complain to. Driver after driver sped past me in air-conditioned ease. After a while I simply ignored all the impassive faces.

As I strode the pavement, the air above it rippled in the intense sunlight. But I had a fine pond to look forward to a few miles ahead. Heat or no, my mood was too upbeat for anything to bother me. What was a little warmth?

At Elbow Lake I found a flimsy, homemade raft that looked like a stage prop left by the forest's original trolls. I bent to work with a 15-foot length of springy, lodgepole pine to pole the shallows and to splash and plunk the few hundred yards to the far end of the lake. Each time I forced the raft forward it dipped half under water.

As shadows lengthened across the forest, I probed along the divide between sun and shade for a good place to swim. The water was as quiet as if it and the firs were frozen forever in an artist's rendition. In that almost palpable silence, something splashed abruptly in the lake's marshy margin. A quick movement drew my attention to a pair of intense button eyes.

I was as still as I have ever been; my muscles ached with the effort. Even the slightest jiggle would have broken the spell.

The sleek swimmer approached the raft slowly. Closer and closer it came, sizing me up and hypnotizing me with its presence. Then in an instant, the opaque water closed over it. I had no time to react; the trance I felt lingered long afterward.

East and west of the Columbia River, hard up on the Canadian border, the forested hills receive few visitors. But that country doesn't need big megafauna and famous places to be important to me. After the mink dove, it, like the Lind Ranch, grew in my imagination.

The forest light was fading. I needed to get off the water to set up camp, cook, and crawl into my sack. But as I poled slowly back to shore, I realized that hiking is full of little moments that don't add up to much in the big scheme of things but which comprise the indefinables that make life worth living. That rough pole in my hand made me feel like a Huck Finn on the Mississippi.

The essence of passing through life is to be able to make memories. Looking back, my *remembered* Elbow Lake has, like that pole, a good heft of emotional weight and significance. Thinking of it makes me happy.

Remembered landscapes are rich with such feelings. My Columbia River country is less a series of GPS waypoints than a series of memories. Whether it is an owl swooping silently out of the night or a mink diving into the depths, I happily return again and again to such moments.

Off the Trail: Longing for Roots

*When you give yourself to places, they give you yourself
back; the more one comes to know them, the more one seeds
them with the invisible crop of memories and associations
that will be waiting for you when you come back, while new
places offer up new thoughts, new possibilities. Exploring
the world is one of the best ways of exploring the mind, and
walking travels both terrains.*
    Rebecca Solnit, *Wanderlust: A History of Walking*, 2000

MOST HIKERS ARE CONTENT with a casual acquaintanceship
with the places that they visit. However, I have been very fortunate
over many decades to return again and again to locales along
the Pacific Northwest Trail, not only to hike them but also to
recruit volunteers to help develop our project. The richness of
that cumulative experience was nowhere more apparent than in
northwest Montana's Yaak River Valley. It was homesteaded early
in the twentieth century, but is still mostly national forest. The
nearest towns are Troy and Libby, forty miles away. In the whole
valley, the only approximation of a post office is a log cabin with
an American flag out front and mailboxes inside. This Rat Creek
"federal building" has no postmaster, but that suits border folks
just fine.

I already knew the Yaak pretty well by the time my hiking buddy
Ted Hitzroth and I marched into the valley on foot in 1983 as part
of our 1,200-mile PNT thru-hike. Searching for local volunteer
Linda Stehlik, we passed a gaggle of dusty pick-ups and tricked-out
Harleys, and found her inside the Dirty Shame Saloon. After we had
caught up on each other's lives, I eavesdropped on conversations
about the depressed state of the area's logging economy. Linda said
that if you could identify the merrymakers in the photos tacked on
the barroom's walls, you'd realize that most of them had already
moved out of the Yaak to find work.

Linda was a woodswoman, wife, and mom whose passion for animals often included a team of Siberian huskies as well as pet porcupines, beavers, and mountain lions. From the Shame, she had a good view across Troy Road to the Yaak Mercantile's porch. Nursing her beer, she nodded toward six young hikers there and asked, "Do you know them?"

"Not yet," I said. "But let's go introduce ourselves." It was obvious from their bulging packs, farmer tans, and wiry builds that they were long-distance hikers. As thrus often do, Ted and I bonded immediately with the strangers. We were talking nonstop at each other when Linda and her husband interrupted to invite us all out to their ranch for dinner. So we piled into the back of Dick's ancient dump truck and went home with our new trail angels.

Bald, soft-spoken Dick Stehlik was a Michigan auto mechanic who'd come into the country in the 1960s. He'd run a gas station, logged small Forest Service contracts, and custom welded. He was a resourceful make-do fellow with a doting, tolerant smile for his young wife's ark of pets. Without hesitation he and Linda welcomed everyone into their cabin to repack, wash, shower, and eat.

The Stehliks were country people with healthy appetites themselves. But their eyes opened wide with amazement when they saw their grub vanish down our ravenous craws. Dick and Linda had not realized that distance hikers gorge like bears preparing for winter. On the trail, we salivate over past pig-outs and dream of future gutbusters. ("All-you-can-eat" is our highest term of culinary praise.) I felt guilty about not warning our hosts that we might clean them out down to their last crumbs.

WHEN I VISITED the Stehliks years later we laughed about that, and Linda discussed her no-frills lifestyle of living off the grid. "We are fortunate," she said, "to have low expenses and plentiful solar panels. Except for a couple of young sled dogs, there is nothing much that I really want."

Dick added, "New people often envy our pretty land here in the valley. But they don't appreciate the sacrifices that went into getting this place. A lot of years, things were pretty thin."

The highlight of that visit came when my friends took me to attend a community hearing about a Forest Service planning report at the log-built community center. It was mid-January. There were flurries outside and hot tempers within. About half the Yaak's two hundred permanent residents had arrived to debate the agency's far-reaching plan for the entire upper Columbia River basin. The hall was full of dour Yaakers who feared that the plan might adversely impact logging.

Hollywood-handsome, a fourth-generation logger complained that reading the government's indigestible document was "like taking a bite out of an elephant." He warned that the agency's preferred alternative would decimate timber jobs. "Ecosystem restoration will close down the woods," he said.

A county commissioner and a miner chorused their agreement. Another logger scoffed that he did not want the valley to become a "mini-Aspen." His unstated message was that he and his working class buddies would no longer be welcome if that happened. To me their laments were all very predictable. From Forks, Washington, to northwest Montana, in every natural resource-based part of the PNT, I'd long heard the same resentful dirge.

Frustration levels were rising fast by the time Rick Bass spoke. What would he say, I wondered? The former professional geologist was no ordinary Yaak resident. As everyone knew, he had almost singlehandedly popularized the valley in book after book, beginning in 1991 with his bestseller, *Winter: Notes From Montana*. In diary format, the then-twenty-nine-year-old visitor from Texas had described his eager anticipation to experience snow and silence: "I knew nothing about winter," he said, "I had never seen it before; and I felt dizzy with fear, giddy with wonder, anticipating it." Bass's tale of that 1987/1988 season was alive with the ebullience of youth. His Yaak months glided across the calendar on magic skates. *Winter* was a love story of man and woman, and of man and his place in the universe. And it and Rick's subsequent pro-environment books were not popular with the locals.

As a *Winter* fan myself, I was delighted that its author had come. Looking resolutely ordinary, he wore a long-sleeved undershirt that peeked out from beneath a white T-shirt. Glum in photos, here he seemed resigned; his sharp arrow of a nose was a directional blaze toward a future that few in the room wanted. When he rose to speak, he said, "It doesn't have to be just recreation or logging. We could have both." I was impressed that he even made the effort to convince such a hostile crowd. After all, mining, logging, and ranching had always been the dominant Montana mindset. People instinctively equated his wilderness message with loss of livelihoods.

My feelings were ambivalent. I understood everyone's fear because I remembered it from when my father had been forced into exile after the collapse of Rhode Island's textile mills. On the other hand, wilderness had been one of my own passions ever since my late twenties.

When the meeting was over, I, like the gal at the dance, prepared to go home with the ones that brung me. But out of the corner of my eye I saw a millionaire landowner, a recent immigrant from Southern California, shaking his fists at Rick and working himself into a frenzy. "Rick, you're the lyingest SOB," yelled the Squire (who I knew to be a radical proponent of unlimited snowmobiling, four-wheeling, and mechanized mayhem). "I know exactly what you're after with your crap." He towered over the writer. "You won't say in public what you say in print. You want *wilderness*. You want people out of the Yaak."

Rick replied evenly, "Where have I ever said that I want people out of the Yaak?"

"You're lying!" the Squire shouted. "Your books say that I can't do what I want to do in the woods. You affect my rights but what are you going to give up?"

"No, I just want to have wilderness," said Rick sadly.

"To be honest," he said, "I think you are a *Socialist*!" That epithet was mild compared to the churlish Squire's next attacks.

Rick protested calmly, "It's not good for you to call me names. I'd like to meet with you regularly to talk this over."

I gazed at the diffident little Texan in disbelief as he held his ground.

The Squire shot back, "I've watched my rights steadily get taken away by you." As his insults accelerated, I was afraid that the big, fifty-seven-year-old galoot was about to slug Rick.

But he didn't. And later all he could do was sputter to anyone who would listen, "What has Bass ever done? He is just a writer!"

I have never forgotten those words. He spat them out as if they were the world's vilest curse. However, their effect for me was to elevate that evening into a kind of morality play about the role of intellectuals in American civic life. At that moment the hall grew crowded with the ghosts of the Transcendentalists, Beats, and other critics of mainstream America. "Just a writer" sounded like high praise to me.

THE PUBLIC HEARING was inconclusive, as such things usually are. But it highlighted the land use pressures that increasingly affected the Pacific Northwest Trail and, indeed, the entire region. In the Yaak, except for a few homesteads patented early in the last century, there is very little private land. Those few parcels will shape the valley's future. And that was what I wanted to discuss with Rick Bass when I later met him at the rental home of some impoverished idealists.

Sherrie and Scott were a fresh-scrubbed pair from Pennsylvania who'd come west after reading *Winter*. She was a massage therapist with no job save occasional babysitting and he was a new activist for Rick's nascent Yaak Valley Forest Council. The twenty-five-year-old Scott was so eager to remain in the valley that he planned to pay $3,500 to a promoter for the right to raise medicinal tree mushrooms. I thought to myself, *Well, why not?* Rick Bass's *Winter* had ended with its author vowing never to leave paradise, and now he owned a quarter section and was doing very well, thank you.

That evening in good light, Rick looked older and more wiry than I'd expected. He was now almost forty (and mentioned that fact several times). His skin was pallid. When deep in thought, he ran his hand across his balding thatch of brown hair. After the wine loosened our tongues, he admitted that he did a lot of soul searching about popularizing the valley. He said, "Everyone here wishes that the Yaak would remain just the way it was when he or she first arrived." He motioned to the newcomers, "They will wish in ten years that their good old days, now, had not changed."

I felt attuned to Rick Bass's romantic view of the Yaak Valley because at heart he and I were brothers in spirit. I was, after all, the dreamer who lived nomadically to promote an unlikely 1,200-mile trail. But the radical changes going on in the valley convinced me that when its large parcels of private land were subdivided, as they surely would be, its character would change forever. Already business at the Merc had picked up from Seattle *weekenders*. There would inevitably be a lot more newcomers like Rick Bass and the Squire who would drive through and want to stay.

Rick told me that he didn't want the Yaak's funky lifestyle to disappear. "There is a lot of the cantankerous hermit in me," he said with a rare smile. "And I am very conservative about new things such as the Pacific Northwest Trail because I feel such a deep respect for the animals. If I happen to disturb a bull elk, he can jump easily into the thickest brush where, even when I was in my twenties, I could not have crawled after him. I feel such an awe for that."

I would have been much more convinced about his "deep respect" if I hadn't known about his passion for killing them. But I said nothing and continued to listen. "I did not fit in here when I first came," he said. "But this country shapes the people, and those that don't fit will leave. It's a tough, unforgiving country. So pieces of me fell away and I developed new pieces. Now I cannot imagine being at home anywhere else."

That was the essence of the situation right there: "I cannot imagine being at home anywhere else." In retrospect, what I remember most from that long-ago confrontation at the Yaak community center was that I never revealed my own deepest feelings. I was as nomadic as the most restless Bedouin, but I sorely envied the rootedness of both Rick Bass and his nemesis the Squire. Unlike me, each man had found his adoptive home and had settled in. Rick Bass, self-proclaimed "most hated man in the largest county in the United States," had thoroughly identified himself with the Yaak Valley. The Squire, for all his egregious faults, also loved the exact same terrain.

That winter, witness to two men's intense passion for place, I could only ask myself, *Will I, too, ever belong somewhere so thoroughly and so happily?*

Solo

... for a month or more, solo walking is best. The pleasures are limitless. You can walk 25 miles a day or you can walk 2 miles a day and it doesn't matter because you can do as you please. I really dug it.

Reid Cross, Pacific Northwest Trail pioneer
letter to the author, August 21, 1975

I AM NOT BY NATURE a hermit, but during years of exploring the Pacific Northwest Trail I often hiked alone with only my shadow for company. When not actually on the trail, I usually lived solo near new sections to further their development. Though I was enviously free of constraints, loneliness sometimes flavored my nomadic life. That begs the question of why I often hike solo.

The reasons are simple enough. I am so used to it that going alone is less a conscious choice than a lifestyle. And what seem like hardships to inexperienced hikers (e.g., bugs and blisters) are nothing special to me. Hunger, exhaustion, and thirst come and go. Ultimately I love hiking by myself because that is when I am closest to total immersion in Nature and to the peacefulness that that affords me.

However, being alone goes against the grain of modern life. From the earliest age, we are taught to be "team players." The vast commerce of entertainment insulates us against the intrusion of self. Although we enter and leave the world on our own, in the interim we are as social as wolves. We congregate in families and work places. We build cities. We identify as tribes or nations. Most people would rather roll in poison ivy than walk by themselves into the unknown.

But I can attest to the fact that a high proportion of long-distance walkers are solitaries. Writing about his 1970 Pacific Crest Trail end-to-end journey, Eric Ryback said:

I had undergone a serious transformation. The shy and wary boy who had rested beside Monument 78 now sat, over 2,300 miles away, sharing himself openly and warmly with strangers who had quickly become friends, with men who had accepted him without hesitation as an equal and colleague. The innocent boy who had trusted nature above all else, who had longed for the isolation and purity of nature, had seen his innocence battered into cunning, his trust wrenched into watchfulness and suspicion, and his misanthropic yearnings exposed as foolish and untenable. I had lost my innocence, but I had found respect—respect for myself, respect for nature, and respect for humanity.

Cindy Ross and Todd Gladfelter usually hike together. But in 1993 they explained the allure of trekking alone in their classic, *A Hiker's Companion*:

A solo hike may be just the thing for doing some soul-searching and reflection. When you are at a crossroads in your life, or are going from one life passage to another, or have a particular problem that needs to be worked out, a solo hike can be an invaluable vehicle in helping you with it. Every year, there are dozens of thru-hikers on the AT who are in exactly that kind of state in their lives—in transition or seeking an answer. Most complete their hike with a much clearer understanding and some wisdom.

My favorite statement of the joy of solo hiking was written in 1975 by a Missouri geology student and PNT pioneer named Reid Cross. He had written to me the previous November hoping to "help to advance the establishment of the trail." While almost completing one of history's very first PNT end-to-end treks he learned more than he had expected about his own capacity for solitary adventuring:

The PNT trip was really something. After I left Oroville, things began to fall into place. I began to get over my loneliness and to enjoy being alone. I guess there is a big difference in being lonely and in being alone. I think that one reason a person seeks the wilderness is to get away from things that bind him in civilization—including his peers. Going with someone is alright for a weekend or even a week but, for a month or more, solo walking is best. The pleasures are limitless. You can walk 25 miles a day or you can walk 2 miles a day and it doesn't matter because you can do as you please. I really dug it.

But consider this contrary view from the author of *Hike Your Own Hike*, Francis Tapon, after his 2007 solo 6,000-mile round-trip on the Continental Divide Trail.

Don't hike alone. You go into the wilderness to leave civilization, but then you realize how important human relationships are. When you come off the trail, you don't talk about what you saw; you talk about the people you met. My CDT yo-yo hike was a metaphor for life. To live a truly fulfilling life you have to create community.

So which shall it be: solo or buddy? The person who hikes by himself is not necessarily a hermit, and the trekker who has company is not necessarily oblivious to the subtleties around her. There are usually multiple ways to reach a destination. In a long, fulfilled life the question is not really solo or together. There are plenty of opportunities for both.

Off the Trail: The Backpacker Parent

*Most people probably think I'm crazy, but I love
[backpacking] with my parents and sister. At home, we're
all too busy to spend extensive time together, but here we
have all the time in the world. We talk, laugh, tell stories,
play games, sing songs, and plan for the upcoming year as
we pass away the miles and take in the scenery ... When life
is slowed down to the speed of a walk, we ... have time to
get to know and to reflect upon ourselves ... When I return,
the only thing that seems to have changed is how skinny I've
become, but truly, the most drastic change is inside me. With
this new view on life, I am ready for anything.*

Danielle Perrot, seventeen years old
PCTA Communicator, December 2005

LIKE SKI BUMS and mountain climbers, we hikers often cobble
together a living in order to indulge our passion. Whenever I
supported myself by housesitting I spent summers on the trail and
the rest of the year wishing for the return of warm weather.

"That's selfish," said those whose focus was on having and
raising children. "What about a mortgage and a career?" said
others. "Get serious," was the naysayers' consensus.

I *was* serious. I learned hiking's greatest lesson—travel lightly—
and I applied it to life off the trail as well. I accumulated remarkably
few possessions. I eschewed debt, and I refused to add another
mouth to the world's hungry billions. Backpacking was what I
liked, and backpacking was what I was going to do.

Life, however, has a sneaky way of throwing curve balls. And in
late 1991 it had the last laugh on child-phobic me.

BY EARLY DECEMBER in Anchorage, I'd completed the manuscript of my book *Alaskans* and was ready to celebrate. So I

popped in out of the cold to visit one of my favorite people, a social worker named Toni. Her heart was as big as Mount Denali, and just then she was obsessing about yet another hard-luck kid. At first I thought she was joking when she pleaded with me to become the child's Christmas caregiver. "Me?" I said. "You've got to be kidding."

But it was no joke. Toni said that several months earlier she'd sent the seriously ill fifteen-year-old Outside (as Alaskans say) to Seattle because Alaska lacked facilities for advanced leukemia care. She assured me that I would only be needed for a very short time until her next real caregiver could be found.

Even I had to admit that it was a compelling story. And I *do* love a good story. *It might not hurt to get some early Christmas spirit,* I told myself, trusting in the obvious fact that no agency would entrust a middle-aged, footloose backpacker with a teenaged girl. I felt perfectly safe in grandstanding, "You can count on me!"

In retrospect, I didn't realize that Toni was desperate to find *anybody* for her Christmas mission. She also knew that I'd long wanted to do some Christmas volunteering. So quicker than I could say, "No, thanks, maybe next year," she had me on a jet to Seattle to spend three weeks at Children's Hospital with a "special needs" kid named Meadow Bloom.

That description—special needs—turned out to be a massive understatement. Leukemia was only the latest in her list of predicaments. At our first meeting, the scrawny, four-and-a-half-foot teen came across as a black hole of personality. Chemo-thinned hair accentuated her impenetrable stare. Someone who'd recently diapered her informed me that she wouldn't need changing for several hours. *Diapered?* How could any child be so jinxed? I sat beside the bed trying to understand the complete otherworldliness of someone with Down syndrome, autism, and such severe retardation that she was incapable of speech.

With great trepidation, I assumed responsibility for "my" charge at the Ronald McDonald House, a cancer patients' hostel that included newborns and teens from as far away as Nome and Boise. I met a little boy who was attached by a tube to an IV pole, a half-dozen bald kids, and a tiny girl with an ugly scar across her head. They and more than a dozen others appeared at my first weekly House meeting. A representative from each family stood to introduce him- or herself. "I am Dena Caterina and I am from Sequim, Washington," said a dark-haired woman. "My son Jeffrey is thirteen years old and he is awaiting a bone marrow transplant."

"I am Jack Brumley and I'm from Victor, Montana," said my neighbor from Room #104. "This is my wife Kelly and our daughter Shelly. Our son Cliffie has a brain tumor and is in the hospital now because his counts are so low from chemo."

Feeling very out of place as a resolute non-parent, I mumbled that I had just arrived from Anchorage to be Meadow Bloom's new caregiver. Everyone seemed to know Meadow and to be at ease with her many afflictions. They were also astonishingly comfortable with medical arcana such as counts, platelets, and Hickman lines (catheters). Ordinary moms and dads nonchalantly discussed blood chemistry as if they were hematology professionals.

Everyone was under extreme stress. Traumatic financial and marital problems were common. And if that were not bad enough, the parents had to swim, often for the first time in their lives, in a group-living fish bowl that exposed everyone's worries and weaknesses.

Of course, my additional challenge was that I had no idea what to do with a regular teenager, never mind one with such severe problems. The closest I'd ever come to being a caregiver was my periodic role minding my mother's two dozen German shepherds and their pups. I felt very out of place when the dining room moms informed me that Meadow was a balky eater who customarily spurned her caregivers' cooking. I sensed them wondering how I would cope. The truth was that I had no idea what I was supposed to serve the child. My own eating habits had developed in countless backcountry camps. Knowing no better, I guessed that teens liked lots of vegetables. In fact, I figured that Meadow Bloom, if she could speak, would probably want my favorite: basic thru-hiker mulligan of greens and ramen.

Families shared tables next to the kitchen. Five-year-old, noodle-loving Cliffie watched solemnly from Meadow's side as I chopped celery, garlic, peppers, carrots, onions, broccoli, and cauliflower. His face was puffy from steroids; his head was bald from chemo; and his brain tumor was essentially hopeless. But he gravitated toward the doll-like Meadow as if drawn by a magnet.

"What's in that thing?" cried the moms when at last I emerged from the kitchen with my campfire-blackened pot, full to the brim with mystery stew. There was no time to explain. Perhaps if I showily ate a few bites myself … Would she catch on? I had to think of something fast because everyone was watching. I placed the battered pot next to Meadow. Steam rose into the air like a benediction as I ladled stew into our bowls.

No one spoke as the child's spoon dipped tentatively into the colorful mess. Little Cliffie watched with the gravity of a very old man. Meadow, impassive, chewed slowly.

She reached for a second spoonful.

And a third.

She finished her bowl.

I brought a second.

Meadow ate four helpings of my lovely stew. The Backpacker Chef was on a roll. From now on it would be noodles and veggies, noodles and more veggies.

THE DIFFERENCES in what we fed our children became a running joke. Meadow ate vegetables; most other kids ate burgers, fries, and pizza. Sometimes the moms challenged me to give Meadow a choice between a glass of prune juice and a glass of Coke. Or a slice of my über-nutritious, homemade Cornell bread versus a piece of greasy, insipid pizza. Because Meadow genuinely preferred fruits and vegetables, she almost always made what I called "the Wise Person's" choice.

Many parents were so distraught that dietary niceties were the farthest thing from their minds. Some of them ate appallingly themselves. What I tried to do was not only to aid Meadow's recovery with good food but also to put some smiles on everyone's faces. Such moments were what I and every other parent at the House lived for. We wanted the children, however ill, to live as normally as possibly. Having brothers and sisters and other relatives of the sick children live with us made the place a true home.

I also very much wanted Meadow, despite her many handicaps, to enjoy "normal" life, as I knew it, until she could recover fully from her leukemia. In practice that meant that the child became a regular participant on my trail-building trips. Whether it was in the middle of the woods or out in a clearcut, Meadow sat in a folding chair, and played one-note, jazz-like, harmonica riffs while my buddies and I moved dirt and cut brush. As time went on, we forgot that there was anything unusual about her participation. She was just part of the crew.

THE HOUSE'S MOMS were always ready with parental advice, but there was one time that I felt that I was way ahead of them. As the manager of Meadow's many capsules, drops, salves, suppositories, and liquids, I found that pills were my trickiest challenge because of their bitter taste. To prevent her from secreting them in her cheeks to spit out later, I began to hide them in grapes (a trick I devised based on having hidden puppies' worming medicine in meatballs). I was very nervous the first time I disguised a small, white methotrexate pill that way. Would she eat it?

No problema! Down it went. In fact, the child was clueless when she happily scarfed a dozen pills in rapid succession. That was the kind of breakthrough that could have earned me a Nobel Prize— if they gave one for childcare. It made me realize why mothers deserve more gratitude and respect than they ever get. But it wasn't as if I had really mastered my parental role. For instance, I had no sooner solved the pills problem than Meadow lost her appetite.

What was worse, she developed such painful constipation that she bawled piteously.

Our nurses and doctors had seen plenty of irregularity, but this case resisted all their nostrums. I longed for the days when Meadow rewarded her success on the throne with giddy applause. Over a week went by with no resolution. The denouement came unexpectedly as Meadow sat in a tub of hot soapy water. As I sponged her down, my thoughts were far away on a piece of trail we'd been building. I was completely unprepared for an underwater feces eruption of such foulness that I fell backward from the tub. In the close confines of that bathroom, I gagged and cried out, "Ack, yech." Distracted by the stench, it took me awhile to notice the grapes that surfaced around the happy child.

After that incident, I carefully staged an experiment to observe Meadow's response to a fresh grape. She promptly ingested it whole the way a pelican would a herring. That was the answer! Her constipation was due to my pill-filled grapes that had stoppered her up as tight as a bung in a barrel.

MEADOW'S PREVIOUS caregiver had taken her everywhere by wheelchair. That surprised me until I began to schlep her to the clinic and stores myself. To dump her into that chair was considerably easier than to lead her patiently by the hand. However, I, as a new parent, wanted the best for "my" child. And just as I did not want Meadow, through my own laziness, to be in diapers, I also did not want her to be immobile. I now knew that I could get her out of the diapers by a strict, two-hour bathroom schedule. Could I free her from the wheelchair, too?

Our House was very conveniently located near many shops. Only three weeks before I'd first arrived, I'd slogged through Anchorage's deep snow. But Seattle's green grass and balmy 40-degree weather encouraged me to test Meadow's scrawny legs on a mini-expedition. House manager Erin Clary was skeptical when I nonchalantly told her that Meadow and I were off for a half-mile walk on the

Burke Gilman Trail. Lacking my enthusiasm for hiking, Erin gave the child a questioning glance. Meadow expressed tacit agreement with my plan by bobbing back and forth.

If I had been lying on my backside for as many months as Miss Bloom had, *I* would have been stiff, too. But the fifteen-year-old put her small left hand in my big right hand and off we trundled. An approach ramp brought us to the former railroad grade. I tugged the girl up that incline like a truck pulling a trailer.

On the trail, the big galoot and the two-feet-shorter shuffler must have looked a sight. We moved very slowly and deliberately. Joggers, cyclists, and strollers passed us in both directions. Halfway along I had to change pulling arms for fear of stretching my right elbow out of joint. I switched Meadow's doll, Clarabell, into her other hand and resumed our march, sensing that Meadow shared my joy to be out in the fresh, mid-winter air. Both my arms felt disjointed by the time we reached a steep eighteen-step stairway down to a shopping strip. Carrying the child made me feel like a real parent because it reminded me of the way my father used to hoist me. And, what the heck, Meadow only weighed half again as much as the large bags of dog food that I used to tote around at my mother's kennels.

That evening Meadow was exhausted from our day on the trail but when I patted her on the head and told her what a good girl she was she squealed with pleasure, which pleased me no end. That reminded me of my own childhood, when my grandmother had lovingly tucked *me* in. I was surprised to find with Meadow that I felt as rewarded from giving attention to her as I had felt comforted by my Nana's love.

After such a long day, when Meadow closed her eyes, her handicaps and illness disappeared into the peace of sleep. As I watched, I was no longer the nomadic writer/hiker, adrift from family life. I felt that I had crossed a threshold to something I could not yet name.

OVER TIME, the Meadow I'd first encountered gave way to someone whose personality was less monochrome. I learned that the child was capable of everything from laughter to hurt. Naturally, I hoped that with patience I might see behind her autistic veil, but there was no dramatic breakthrough. Her back-and-forth rocking and her tuneless riffs continued as before. What did improve was her strength, as we walked miles on the Burke-Gilman Trail and patrolled the co-op's aisles for vegetables, grains, yogurts, and breads. I pulled and directed the cart from the front while she tagged along like a happy caboose. If I stopped to question myself about 4 percent versus non-fat yogurt, Junior rocked judiciously, as if she, too, were weighing what the Wise Person would do.

To go from the wheelchair of December to the walks of spring was major progress. One day, on those same Sandpoint Way stairs, I left her alone at the top, and then called up to her from a few steps farther down to follow me unaided.

Traffic passed noisily. Diesel trucks spat black smoke. For what seemed like forever, she didn't move at all. *Well, it was worth a try,* I thought.

Then Meadow gripped the railing with both hands and looked blankly toward me from the top step. I coaxed, "Okay, Meadow, you can do it." I told her to lower one foot to the next step. "That's good," I said when she unexpectedly did that. "Now lower your other foot," I said, relying on the tone of my voice, as I would with a hesitant pup.

Down went that foot. I watched from two steps below, ready to catch her if she fell. After a couple more steps, I helped for the rest of her descent.

The next morning Meadow took five stairs unaided. By the end of the week, her hesitation had vanished. From then on, she always descended those stairs with confidence.

MEADOW AND I visited the hospital's pediatric oncology clinic several times a week in a routine that was almost cheerily familiar. We made small talk with the receptionist and the families. We loafed about while we waited for the weigh-in and the blood draw. We queued to see a physician.

In the narrow confines of that antechamber I became comfortable with the crying children and the bustling staffers. I liked the place's utilitarian ways and easy friendliness, its mix of love and professionalism. On a typical day I stripped off Meadow's coat and shoes. Nurse Joanne recorded a weight of 32 kilograms in a voluminous file and did a CBC, a complete blood count. Meadow lay comfortably on an examining table while Joanne painlessly extracted a blood sample. Afterward, Meadow and I took it to the laboratory.

Some days Joanne needed a urine sample. So I placed a "hat" receptacle in the toilet bowl for Meadow to fill. If the child felt well, she clapped excitedly at her accomplishment. Often I, too, wanted to applaud the clinic's small acts of courage and compassion that every day went unrecognized. We lived in a drama that played out slowly. I thought of myself as a spectator until the day I woke up to realize that I was part of the cast.

"WHEN WAS THE LAST TIME you washed that thing?" challenged Dena Caterina one evening while I fixed Meadow her supper. While I stir-fried some vegetables, Meadow improvised on her ancient mouth harp.

"I have *never* cleaned it," I said. "Do harmonicas need to be washed?"

Dena was a nurse whose thirteen-year-old son's leukemia had already been "cured" once, relapsed, and undergone a second round of chemotherapy. This time his lack of response to chemo meant that his only hope was a bone-marrow transplant. I knew Jeff's mother as our resident germ-buster. As soon as she peered inside Meadow's instrument she cried, "Yuck! That's a health hazard. These kids have such low counts that this harmonica could kill somebody!"

I revered old-timer Dena as a leukemia expert. And she was physically bigger than I was. So we traipsed into the broom closet while Meadow scarfed vegetables and chugged prune juice. The kid was so single-minded about eating that she didn't even see me filch her beloved mouth harp. I looked at its fine-grained wood, and I looked at Dena's cauldron of acid. She declared again, "You could be infecting the whole house!" She snatched the instrument from me and dropped it into her bucket of bleach and cleansers. "We'll let it soak until it's good and clean," she said.

I knew, as we all did, that Dena's insurance company had refused to pay for her son's bone-marrow transplant. Even if she managed to raise several hundred thousand dollars, she would still need to find a donor whose marrow matched Jeff's. Tête-à-tête with me in the broom closet, she felt free to speak about what was really on her mind: Jeff's poor prognosis. Her voice cracked as she elaborated on the grim details. I listened and listened, unsure what to say. She did not ask me for advice. As a nurse, she understood the medical facts much better than I did. No, what she needed was somebody she could lean on. And I felt completely inadequate.

Any conversation at the House had the potential to veer suddenly into deep waters. This was not the first time that I found myself floundering, way in over my head. I did not know how to respond to Dena's pain. It scared the heck out of me because my own response to death was so inadequate. I had seen people rise to the occasion to be able to comfort the afflicted. However, as a backpacker all I knew was walk, eat, stop, and sleep. The rhythm of trail days was reassuring and unthreatening. In life-and-death situations I was still the greenhorn. Although Pathfinder was my trail name, in that broom closet with Dena I lost my ability to navigate.

THE MOMS WERE not happy that I bought only black shoes, black pants, black shirts, and black hats for Meadow. "But wouldn't she be so adorable in a nice little dress?" they whined.

No, thank you. Black was *practical.* Thanks to Meadow's incontinence and messy eating, I often had to change her several times a day. Of course, the moms didn't buy any of my excuses. They wanted *frilly.* One of them finally accompanied me to a department store to see that I bought something "more suitable for a teenaged girl."

Why is the subject of women's clothing so deliberately mysterious? Why are the sizes so irrational? At the cavernous store, we faced the insoluble issue of whether Meadow qualified as a "junior." Even the saleswomen did not know if four-and-a-half-foot-short Meadow ranked as a large child or a very small woman. Luckily my advisor steered me away from a few spectacular color clashes until I found some sweaters and shirts that, I thought, elevated the teenager from the hoi polloi to the carriage trade. Things went tolerably well until my consultant discovered a "cute" red pullover decorated with appliqued kittens. "They're so irresistible," she gushed. I stared suspiciously at a clutch of misbegotten cats that, God help me, peered out of a flower pot. Our luck held, though, because I simultaneously spotted a children's sweatshirt adorned with the famed Georgetown University bulldog. As soon as I saw it, I immediately forgot my makeover hopes for Junior's new elegance. Here was the jaunty jaw and the spike collar. The nickname "HOYAS" stood out in bold relief on the black cotton. I smiled when I imagined my child recognizing the school's official 1789 seal.

In the end it never mattered at all if Meadow qualified as a "junior." When she rocked back and forth and blew her one-note harmonica riffs in the bulldog shirt, she was as close to perfect for me as anyone could be.

I SPENT A YEAR as Meadow's caregiver. Often that experience was painfully poignant, such as the several times that she almost died of septic shock. Others were so funny that I and the other parents laughed out loud with delight. We all learned that the lifestyle of childhood cancer is less about illness than about living.

Though Meadow recovered from leukemia and returned to Alaska, she relapsed two years later and soon died. Her death profoundly affected many people, each in his or her own way. All I can say is that I now know for sure what I only suspected then: that a person who is off the trail is not necessarily lost. During those twelve months at Children's Hospital I began to feel that *I* was on the right path.

Today certain images—mostly of walking—come to mind whenever I think of Meadow. In the most recurrent scene, I lead my child down a long hospital corridor while people's faces light up at our approach. "Hello, Meadow," they beam. Small children, adoring her, are drawn in like magnets. For a moment even adults forget their worries.

I used to find it difficult to give and to receive love. Meadow Bloom, though incapable of speech or conceptual thought, was a master emotional communicator who drew out the best in everyone, even me. In the end she was one of the best teachers this traveling-light nomad ever had.

Along the PNT: The Selkirk Mountains

*A special buoyancy lit up Randolph [New Hampshire] in
those years [the 1880s]. A small group of lively summer
residents fused with half a dozen local woodsmen-
mountaineers to form a creative alliance for trail work, as
well as an atmosphere crackling with physical vitality and
uproarious good times. Randolph in the eighties was one
of those rare and precious moments in any region's history
when the bloom was fresh and new worlds of enterprise and
adventure were there to be grasped, amid lots of hard work,
camaraderie, and joy.*

Laura and Guy Waterman, *Forest and Crag*, 1989

AS EVIDENCED by the above quote from New Hampshire's
Presidential Range, volunteer trail work has a long and distinguished
history in the United States. That tradition directly informed the
development of the Pacific Northwest Trail. I was exceptionally
lucky to be part of the project when "the bloom was fresh and new
worlds of enterprise and adventure were there to be grasped."

I love to make new country give up its secrets. That was especially
true when I sought to locate the best crossing from the Kootenai
River to Priest Lake across north Idaho's Panhandle. Standing in
my way was a dramatic chain of granitic mountains whose location
on the Canadian border guaranteed that harsh weather beset them
much of the year. Their glacier-polished faces were reminiscent of
California's Yosemite, and there had been talk of creating a new
Selkirk Mountains National Park.

My original 1970s route had utilized the valley of Long Canyon
Creek, which was rich in giant white pines, trout-filled pools, and
primo bottomlands. But eventually I realized that Long Canyon was
not adequate to showcase the grandeur of the Selkirk Mountains.
Now, in 1982, my self-imposed goal was to select the very best *high*

route, even if I had to include some bushwhacking. I settled upon a spectacular new route from the river (at 1880 feet elevation) via the 13-mile Parker Ridge Trail to an elevation of 7670 ft. at Parker Peak. That way was cottonmouth dry except for a spring five miles up. Campsites were few, but the intermittent views of the high country invariably put a bounce in my steps. I hoped future hikers would appreciate the scenery as much as I did.

That 1982 route continued west via Long Mountain and offered grandstand views of the pointy prow of Smith Peak and the granite ramparts of Lions Head. I very much wanted to swing north to follow the Selkirk Crest through some of the Lower 48's finest trail-less country. But as a practical matter, I needed to keep bushwhacking to a minimum by choosing a shorter, southwestward course *across* the Selkirks. At the time I described the resulting 8-mile route from Ball Lakes to Myrtle Peak as "mostly ridgerunning, bushwhacking, and rubbernecking."

From Lower Ball Lake, gain the ridge southwest of the lake by climbing the scree and contouring around Knob 7265'.

Don't bother climbing to the top of this rocky, mostly treeless prominence. Just go high enough to slip around its southeast side to the southward-running ridge beyond. This ridge extends 3.5 miles to Myrtle Peak (7211). Our progress is between and over a series of bumps and knobs, dodging the wind-dwarfed firs, and sometimes hopping from rock to rock. Where you cross the glacier-polished planes of granite, you will be thankful for your Vibram boot soles. This is not a place for missteps.

It wasn't long, however, before I became dissatisfied with that route's lack of directness. So I decided to re-explore its "southward-running ridge" *before* Myrtle Peak to see if I could exit the Selkirks via Lion Creek Pass. Some people think that exploration is a thing of the past because every square mile of the earth's surface has been surveyed by satellites. All I know is that I was excited to return to the remote, broken country in the shadow of the Lions Head to try again to improve the PNT.

Once again I looked back down at Pyramid Lake's dark waters from the bluff trail. Passing granite blocks the size of houses, I climbed to Upper and Lower Ball Lakes in a basin that connected to my next ridge. After a night at the lower lake, I continued my sunny climb beyond the outlet. It was easy to pick my way up through the boulders, sub-alpine firs, whitebark pines, and huckleberries to about the 6900-foot contour. Then I eased around Knob 7265' on slippery, gelid grasses and glacier-gouged shelves of granite.

Sweating by the time I reached Myrtle Ridge, I stripped down to T-shirt and shorts. The early morning light showcased the fir-green crease of Long Canyon as it swung toward me from the northeast. Across the verdant valley, Lions Head's crenellated bulwark stood brightly against the horizon. And in the other direction, my ridge rippled toward the southern Selkirks. Where, I wondered, could I bushwhack down off my sky island to Lion Creek Pass? The topo hinted at a relatively moderate descent up ahead.

But when I arrived at what seemed to be the correct spot, its vertiginous, green drop was surprisingly abrupt. No matter, for the first time that day I stopped navigating long enough to enjoy the sense of freedom that I always find in places no one else wants.

Okay, this is it, I thought to myself when I identified a likely timber finger down through the cliffs. *No place to make a mistake.* I took a bearing on Lion Creek Pass, a thousand feet below. That glorious scenery of convoluted peaks and valleys made me so happy that I let out a wild shout before dropping over the edge into the thick brush. Alders and dog fir helped to brake my descent as I picked my way through random openings, first one way, then another. Sometimes I followed small trickles and seeps where they made for easier going.

I wanted to hit Lion Creek Pass just right, not only to learn what was there but also to avoid unnecessary floundering in the headwaters country to either side of my goal. Sometimes I fell into holes. Thorns skinned my fingers. Sticks poked and bloodied my bare legs.

Lion Creek Pass turned out to consist of a park-like setting of tall firs where expanses of *Menziesia ferruginea* (fool's huckleberry) glowed in the intervals between trees. All that remained was to bushwhack west down the trail-less north fork of Lion Creek toward Priest Lake.

I was overjoyed to have found my Selkirks passage. Thinking about that route's mental and physical challenges still makes me smile. Trail location in the 1980s Selkirks (as in the 1880s Presidential Range) was indeed full of "new worlds of enterprise and adventure."

Of course that was yesterday. What are the further opportunities for developing outstanding long distance trails? I firmly believe that for years to come anyone with gumption and skill will be able to locate and develop magnificent trails.

I feel very confident that the best is yet ahead.

Women on the Trail

I love all parts of being out there on the trail, such as the
excitement when the sun comes out after a couple days of
rain—or a week of it. My mom took me on my first hiking
trip when I was eleven. It was a disaster, but I was hooked.
There is nothing better for building self-confidence than
deciding to do 26 miles and then doing them: getting into
camp sweaty and disgusting but proud.

Faren "Castle" MacDonald, twenty-three years old
solo thru-hiker, Appalachian Trail, 2009

ONE OF THE TRAIL world's most encouraging developments has
been the gradual increase in the number of women hikers. And why
not? As my friend Triple Crown hiker Melanie Simmerman says,
"There is little difference between why men hike and why women
do. Not enough is made of the fact that women like adventure and
physical and mental challenge."

This chapter profiles three exemplary women hikers. Their
approaches to the sport differ, but what unites Sheila Pearson, Clare
Cain, and Deb Levine is that each thoroughly accepts the notion
that the hiking world is her domain to enjoy to the maximum of
her ability.

I look forward to the day when there are such huge numbers of
distaff hikers that I will have to write a chapter about a new hiking
minority called "Men on the Trail."

SHEILA PEARSON (1963–) didn't fit the sport's physically fit
twenty-something stereotype when she joined her husband in 2004
to thru-hike the PCT. Neither she nor Tom Pearson was out to
break any speed records; they were middle-aged and they knew
it. In fact, two years earlier, Sheila, then thirty-eight, had weighed
a whopping 284 pounds when Tom, then fifty-four, asked her to

make the trek. Lacking any hiking experience whatsoever, her first reaction was, "Oh my God, I can't walk 25 miles a day! Are you crazy?"

Sheila had married Tom a decade after he took lessons from her at a dance studio. But it was clearly quite a jump to waltz to Canada on the PCT. She only agreed after reading about a couple who honeymooned on the trail. Rachel and Scott Kimler's experiences inspired Sheila to begin to think that she, too, could go the distance.

Sheila and Tom spent two years building up their endurance for the five-month trek. In the process, Sheila lost 80 pounds. Then in 2004, while end-to-ending the Crest Trail's 2,600 miles, she lost another 54 pounds, for a grand total of 134 pounds. In other words, almost half of the original Sheila Pearson disappeared. In its place was a new sense of life's possibilities gained from living on the trail. "The only real worries," she said, "were locating enough water for the day (or two if it was a dry stretch), eating enough to maintain strength, and figuring out where to camp for the night. Yes, we had to plan resupply carefully, but once we were on the trail, life was *sweet* (even if I had hissy fits when I got tired)."

Long-distance walkers are a restless breed, infected by knowledge of an alternative life that exists *out there*. Sheila, having hiked the PCT, soon began to dream of another thru-hike. "When we finished, I said 'never again' because I had no feeling in my toes. But, three weeks after re-entry, I was searching the AT's Web sites for information. I guess thru-hiking is an itch; once you have it, you have to scratch it again and again. Non-hikers can't understand that I thrive on digging cat holes, sleeping on the ground, and walking incomprehensible distances through beautiful country while eating a limited variety of food."

Recently I asked Sheila what advice she would give to anyone contemplating a thru-hike. She replied vehemently:

Just do it! I honestly think that if I can manage a thru-hike,
then anyone can. Do your homework, learn as much as you

*can about where you're going to hike, make a plan, and
then be prepared for it to change. Flexibility is your friend
over a long hike because there are so many factors involved.
Injuries, illness, trail conditions, and fatigue are only a few.
Listen to your body, and keep your gear light and multi-
functional, because you won't need as much as you thought
and because hiking is more pleasurable with a lighter load.*

Sheila believes that the most common mistake that new hikers
make is having exaggerated expectations at the beginning of a long
hike about what their bodies will tolerate. She says:

*We had to ease our way into Big Miles on the PCT because
of my previous back and leg injuries. Our philosophy
was necessarily Start Slow and Taper Off—which became
our trail names. If you start out too fast, you are almost
guaranteed to get shin splints, fractures and blisters. Start
out doing short day hikes close to home without a pack then
move on to carrying a pack, then go out for a couple days
with a light load. In other words, do a shakedown hike to
determine what gear you really need and what food you
truly like. Listen to your body. If you get a hot spot, stop
and take care of it unless you like blisters. If you're tired,
stop, rest, and eat something. Keep hydrated. Sometimes all
it takes is ten or fifteen minutes to feel rejuvenated again.*

Whenever I asked Sheila what she had *gained* from hiking her
answers always involved hardships in places such as Washington's
Goat Rocks:

*The three miles of high, totally exposed, steep ridges in the
Goat Rocks Wilderness are no place to be at night during a
white out. We miscalculated our hiking speed and got stuck
on the most exposed section between 8 p.m. and midnight
as a storm pressed in. My light was buried in my pack, and
Tom only had a small light attached to his trekking pole.*

During the endless hours that he slowly guided us over those long miles, I was a mess. In almost total darkness, all I could do was to stumble along, stepping diligently in each of his tracks to make certain that I was following him. I trusted him to get us down safely; I just didn't trust myself. One misstep could have been disastrous.

After experiences like that, Sheila threatened to go home at nearly every remaining town. But she never did quit, and in the process she made the transition from a 284-pound non-hiker to a PCT veteran. I had asked what she had gained from hiking. Her answer was, "Know your own limitations and pace yourself accordingly."

I applaud Sheila for never letting the tough times define the hike for her. She built up her physical stamina and her mental toughness until she could accept the inevitable setbacks enough to keep on going. If I could, I would arrange for her to tell her story to every women's group in the country.

CLARE CAIN (1977–) is lucky in that she is able to combine her hiking avocation with her paid employment. She is the very able director of trail stewardship for the Connecticut Forest and Park Association.

Hiking means primarily simplicity to Clare. She says, "I crave the dream state that I sometimes slip into when hiking. Hours pass, and I don't even remember the mountain I just went over. At those times, walking is intensely meditative. Step after step, mile after mile, day after day, the worries of the world dissolve and my mind seems to expand. Memories from long ago come flooding back, and the simple repetition of walking steals me away."

Clare is accustomed to working long hours as a trail club administrator. But like many introverts, she feels that her "most natural" self only surfaces when she is covered with trail grime and is walking toward the horizon. She thrives on the challenges of

bad weather, sore feet, and deep fatigue. She says of her 2008 Long
Trail thru-hike, "It rained seventeen out of nineteen days, and I
almost never saw a view. The terrain was slick and treacherous;
the mud was often knee-deep. Yet, when I think back, I absolutely
loved it because nothing was contrived. The struggle was pure;
the weather and the mountains were dominant. My body was in
perfect balance. The food I ate was directly absorbed and turned
into energy to walk without excess or toxins. It was as if I sweated
away all of life's impurities." Clare is unusual as a long-distance
hiker in that she also knows the trail world from the perspective of
a manager, first of the North Country Trail and now of the New
England Trail. She says:

*The opportunity simply to walk, surrounded by untouched
pockets of the natural world, is such an undervalued part
of our society. If I hadn't had the escape of local trails and
woods as a kid, I wouldn't be who I am today. Working in
a professional capacity to provide such opportunities for
others is a special honor. Our National Trails are where
anyone can seek adventure, escape stress, and experience
life without excess. Out on the trail, simplicity prevails and
humility is required.*

Clare is a thru-hiker (AT, 1999; LT, 2008) who oversees maintenance of 825 miles of blue-blazed pathways. Because hiking
makes her feel "grounded in the natural world" she approaches
her job with passion, creativity, and happiness.

THE DAY HIKER is the most important person on our trails. Yes,
the thrus get all the publicity and attention, but the plain fact is
that well over 90 percent of trail travel is by short-distance users.
So what exactly is a day hiker?

Rather than give a sure-to-be-contradicted definition, I am
putting forward DEB LEVINE (1952–) as the archetypal example.
Like so many people she developed a love for woods tramping

in childhood. She grew up with hiking in her life though not in any formal or organized way. "Then in college," she says, "my adventures became a little bit longer and my mountains a little bit higher. But my outings were always day trips."

For a long time after that she felt that she ought to try backpacking because there would surely be so much more to experience if she camped overnight and woke up on the trail ready for another day of walking. However, her busy schedule and competing interests always got in the way.

Eventually she realized that carrying a small, light pack suited her needs. "When I am out for a day I can break free of mundane matters to feel the awe and joy of being in beautiful, natural places," she says. "I feel a personal sense of achievement when I set a goal and then meet it (and then have a comfortable bed to sleep in at night)."

Deb's love of day hiking recently expressed itself in a year spent as volunteer leader of the Berkshire Chapter of the Appalachian Mountain Club (AMC). She says:

I believe that we women often find ourselves burdened with so many responsibilities and shoulds in our lives that we don't make time for ourselves. That's why trail club activities are incredibly freeing for me emotionally, spiritually, and physically. Our day hikes reconnect me with a deeper sense of self. Being in nature—whether it is a full day or just a couple of hours—is essential to remembering what is valuable in my life.

Deb also loves the sense of comradery that she gets from hiking with her club. "Sharing the trail with like-minded folks, experiencing our adventures and sometimes misadventures: I would not trade that feeling of connection and fun for anything." That bond with other hikers was what led Deb to become more deeply involved with the AMC and to follow the example of its many men and women who still make day hiking a regular part of their lives well into their seventies and eighties.

If, as is true, the future of America's trails depends on our many trail-maintaining organizations, then the prosperity of those groups will rest upon the shoulders of day hikers like Deb Levine. It is the people who actually do the work who make our trails possible. And it is from the ranks of day hikers that future volunteers will come.

I CAN ONLY GUESS what keeps some women off the trails. But I know that many women are out there enjoying themselves to the utmost. Their motivations are not perceptively different than men's. In a sport with few rules, each woman will make of it what she wants. It needn't be competitive or noncompetitive, fast or slow, long or short. Therein lies its beauty.

Pass It On

It is likely that you get e-mails like this one all the time—
that is, e-mails from people aspiring to be the first successful
Sea-to-Sea thru-hiker. Nevertheless, please read this one with
care because it could result in a life-changing event.
Andrew Skurka, letter to the author, March 30, 2003

MENTORING TAKES many forms: giving specific suggestions, sharing experience, or, sometimes, just exuding confidence in someone. It takes time because it is primarily about caring.

Whatever success we have in life often comes from standing on the shoulders of those who came before us. A wise person understands that debt and tries to repay it by passing the favor on to someone else.

As I said earlier, back when I was a green kid in 1970, I contacted Harvey Manning about my plans to hike east to west across the North Cascades. After that hike, I showcased my adventures in a poorly written article that was, I thought (with the assurance of youth), guaranteed to win prompt public support for creation of a new long-distance trail. Harvey could have ignored me, but instead he sent long, generous letters to encourage me to pursue my dream:

I very much enjoyed receiving your piece, and I hope to
see you again this summer. But since we are really "good
friends of the trail," even though we haven't met or talked
often, may I offer the critique of a friend? Frankly, I was
disappointed. I think you got off on the wrong foot in the
writing. You have not conveyed, in the article [about the
proposed trail] the sense of excitement, of pioneering, you
conveyed to me in our conversations.

What he no doubt meant was that the turgid style that I'd developed in graduate school was inadequate for a book meant to convince the public to support a new, untested project. Nevertheless, I was delighted when Harvey wrote two months later after my latest effort that, "I felt before, and know now for certain, that you can do the subject abundant justice." 1972 brought more encouragement. I still remember the glow I felt when he said of my again-revised manuscript: "I thoroughly enjoyed hiking along with you. It's all country I know, and you've got it down right. One of the great strengths of the book will be the human encounters—the cross-section of wilderness travelers at this point in time."

I LOVE TO ASK people about their mentors because the answers are often so surprising. In 2001 Flyin' Brian Robinson hiked 7,371 miles in three hundred days to become the first person to complete the Pacific Crest Trail, Continental Divide Trail, and Appalachian Trail all in one year: backpacking's "Calendar Triple Crown." He told me recently:

> *I credit my father and my Boy Scout Troop for fostering my love of hiking and backpacking, but I can't really credit either with mentoring me. Most of what they taught me I've had to unlearn along the way. I've grown more through personal experience and research rather than a mentorship. I've definitely been a mentor though. My Dad was my first student. He introduced me to backpacking, but I introduced him to thru-hiking.*

Brian's father, Roy (who hiked the PCT in 1999, the AT in 2002), acknowledged that debt but said that the long trails themselves are the ultimate beneficiaries from our mentoring. "They will continue to exist," he said, "only so long as we and future generations use and value them. If we and our sons and daughters don't actively protect our national scenic trails, they will be lost forever." Of course, I agreed with Roy completely. I even know one young person who can illustrate his point.

IN 1996, I PROPOSED linking certain long-distance trails into a new route across the northern U.S. that would give at least a semblance of unity to the helter-skelter National Trails System. I described this plan in the magazine of the Pacific Northwest Trail Association:

> *My own latest dream is to think of our Pacific Northwest Trail as but the beginning of a coast-to-coast trail. The route would include: the PNT; the Continental Divide Trail; the North Country Trail; the Long Path; the Appalachian Trail; and the International Appalachian Trail. Thus the coast-to-coast route would begin at Cape Alava on the Pacific Ocean and end on the Gaspé Peninsula at the Atlantic Ocean. Impractical, impossible? No. North America needs a first class east-west route. And all of us need big dreams to give life just that much more zest!*

My attempt to extrapolate the PNT east to the Atlantic Ocean gained a boost in February 2003 when *Backpacker Magazine* published an article about my transcontinental Sea-To-Sea Route (C2C). At the time I was simply intent upon improving the National

Trails System by giving it a sort of backbone across the northern tier of Lower 48 states. I don't think it ever occurred to me that anyone would want to thru-hike C2C all in one shot. After all, its 7,700-mile length was, I thought, prohibitively long and its route was usually snowbound.

However, would-be C2C pioneers surprised me with their enthusiasm. I remember my astonishment that spring when I received an out-of-the-blue message from a college senior named Andrew Skurka. Like me three decades earlier, he was obviously in thrall to exploratory desire:

> *March 30, 2003*
> *Mr. Strickland,*
> *It is likely that you get e-mails like this one all the time—that is, e-mails from people aspiring to be the first successful Sea-to-Sea thru-hiker. Nevertheless, please read this one with care because it could result in a life-changing event. I am a senior at Duke University in Durham, NC, and will graduate in December 2003. Last summer, at the age of twenty-one, I hiked the entire Appalachian Trail in ninety-five days, averaging almost 23 miles per day. After finishing the AT, I immediately began to think about my next trail, and the PCT became tops on my list—until I read about the Sea-to-Sea Route in* Backpacker. *I would classify the C2C as a "wild idea" of mine at this point—something I am strongly lured to in the abstract, for four reasons:*
> *1. It would be another "ultimate test" of my mental strength.*
> *2. Long-distance hiking is a great way to see the country.*
> *3. It would result in numerous endorsements and launch my career as a professional backpacker, mountaineer, guide, outfitters manager, etc.*
> *4. It would draw attention to our national scenic trails, possibly resulting in federal designation for the C2C.*

But here is the catch: I am clueless in the details (e.g., restocking, weather, trail conditions, etc.) and do not know where to start.

A prompt response would be greatly appreciated. I may need to start planning.

Thanks,

Andy

Long before young Skurka's query, eager beavers used to send me similar letters about the Pacific Northwest Trail. Most of those dreamers soon thought better of it, or, if they began the trail, didn't finish. (Eventually four Oregonians—the first of many PNT thrus—completed every bit of its 1,200 miles in 1977.*) Three decades later, C2C was over six times longer and very much more of a navigational/logistical puzzle. Nevertheless, though I expected that young Skurka's enthusiasm would evaporate like the morning mists, I sent an encouraging response.

Of course, twenty-something Andrew Skurka no more needed help in 2004 with C2C than had twenty-something Ron Strickland in 1970 with the PNT. Both young men were buoyed up with an indomitable determination. Skurka later explained, "The *Backpacker* article absolutely inspired me, and before I even finished reading it I had pretty much decided what I was going to do when I finally graduated in December."

On October 20, 2003, he reported that he was happy with his initial fund-raising but distressed by the previous night's conversation with his mother. "She thinks the C2C is dangerous and does not make sense," he wrote in an e-mail. "She's slightly correct on the first part, especially in the remote sections and in the early spring and late fall. I disagree with the second part, though, and will need to work on changing her opinion."

*Janet Garner and Rex Bakel were the first team; the second comprised Scott Shuey and Jerry Smith, plus non-Oregonian Heath Hibbard.

Karen Skurka began to realize just how serious her son was about his cockeyed plan when he spent months listing every detail of his upcoming 7,700-mile hike on an Excel spreadsheet. Most people tend to be flummoxed by planning for even a simple weekend overnighter. But three-fifths of Andy's route, the North Country National Scenic Trail, had no guidebook; many sections had not yet even been built. The Sea-to-Sea Route thru-hike was, to put it mildly, a daunting, over-the-top conceptual and physical challenge. But Karen's determined son approached each problem methodically.

On August 6, 2004, Andrew set off from Cape Gaspé, Quebec, at the mouth of the St. Lawrence River to hike to the Pacific Ocean. Following the sketchy International Appalachian Trail, he kept going through New Brunswick and Maine to the Appalachian Trail. After New Hampshire and Vermont, the 4,600-mile North Country Trail took him through New York, Pennsylvania, Ohio, and Michigan. Even though I was responsible for having inspired his trek, I was still astonished by his speed under grueling conditions. With his mother as his base camp for laundry and food drops, Skurka seemed determined to do the impossible. His Web site (also maintained by his mom) explained that he was carrying a tiny vial of Atlantic Ocean water as "a daily reminder of the ultimate objective" of his journey: to pour it over his head when he reached the Pacific.

Despite having often talked and corresponded with him, I had never met Andrew face-to-face. In late December, he took a short Christmas break from hiking at his parents' Seekonk, Massachusetts, home. I was eager to discuss his progress, but when I visited for dinner, I realized that his mom still thought C2C was crazy and that I was a Pied Piper of irresponsibility. We waited for Bob Skurka to come home from work while Karen prepared dinner in her flowered-wallpaper kitchen. Her fresh-faced, outgoing, all-American kid was so unselfconscious that he happily contorted himself on the floor in stretching exercises while he talked C2C with me and bantered good-naturedly with her. With the arrival of his dad, we all chatted politely about Rhode Island's native foods, since the Skurkas, like me, had grown up in that nearby culinary mecca.

Despite Karen and Bob's attempts at civility, the tension was palpable throughout dinner. They grieved in advance at the prospect of their only son's returning to deepest winter in upstate Michigan. Why should anyone, they seemed to ask, walk straight into the path of horrific blizzards on a harebrained cross-country trek for no possible gain?

I knew that Andrew had originally been "totally on a corporate track at Duke." So I wasn't surprised during dessert when his banker father Bob repeatedly grilled me about the possibilities for gainful employment "in the backpacking field." He had expected that his son would make something of himself by putting his degree (Political Science and Economics) to use in investment banking. I felt so sorry for him that I genuinely tried to concoct a C2C rationalization to justify Andy's louche plans. But each time I warmed to my hopeless task I could hardly keep a straight face because Andy kept hiding more of the carrots that his mom expected him to eat.

After dinner I took a photo of the aggrieved parents and their beaming son beside a map of the Sea-to-Sea Route. I was the oldest person present (by over a decade), and I felt like a heel.

During the next half-year, Karen continued to act as her son's base camp, mailing food drops to him and washing his smelly laundry. Despite her very real fears, she supported her son when he most needed help.

Over the course of eleven months and 7,778 miles, often snowshoeing in temperatures so cold that his flask of North Atlantic water froze in his pack, Andrew Skurka thru-hiked C2C across North America. Finally, after 301 days of walking, he unfurled his Explorers Club flag at Cape Alava on the Olympic Peninsula, stood in the surf, and poured that vial of Atlantic Ocean water over his head.

In naming him its 2005 "Person of the Year," *Backpacker Magazine* said:

> *Conquering the [C2C] route alone merits genuflection, but that's not why Skurka made our cut. It's his approach: He didn't do it to option movie rights, or to create legions of paying Skurka disciples. He did it, he told us from a pay phone somewhere in the heartland, because "it gives people a sense of the great potential of a national trail system." Where most thru-hikers are inwardly focused, avoiding outside contact except to resupply, Skurka makes time to talk with Boy Scouts, senior citizens, trail clubs, and school groups and remind them that their local trails not only serve their recreational needs but also link them to a larger community.*

Andrew subsequently described his adventures in public lectures in every part of the country. *National Geographic Adventure Magazine* named him its 2007 "Adventurer of the Year" after a further epic trek, a 6,875-mile foot tour of the wilderness West. In 2010, sponsored by National Geographic, he completed an astonishing, self-propelled circumnavigation of Alaska.

One of the many things that I admire about Andrew Skurka is that he is so good at influencing young people to think positively about hiking. Though his own teenaged experiences in the woods were limited to a few family camping trips, he has become a stellar role model for passionate involvement in Nature. Best of all, his fans can be found among people of all ages.

I WISH I HAD BEEN with Jay Zitter when she met fellow moms Sharon and Jacqui on a perfect October morning for a work trip in the heart of New York's Finger Lakes region. Jay remembers: "A slender young man suddenly materialized wearing an orange plastic rain slicker, an 11-pound pack, and an irresistible ear-to-ear grin. He said he was walking our entire North Country Trail. We liked him because he looked so young and because he always sent his clothes home for his mother to wash." In 2004, Jay and her friends had never seen an actual thru-hiker when Andrew Skurka appeared in their midst like a genie from a bottle.

Using e-mail and phone calls, Jay and others passed Andrew along from one NCT chapter to the next. Kay Kujawa of Rudyard, Michigan, remembers putting Andrew up one very cold winter night after the lad had snowshoed 18 miles through soft slushy snow, sinking 18 inches with each step.

He came in just at dusk and left before full light the next morning. There we were, two seniors living out in the middle of nowhere, and in stepped this well-mannered and genteel young man to spend the night with us. Before dinner he spent an hour doing stretching exercises and telling us about his trip. Let me tell you, he was one hungry fellow. We raised two sons so we know how much boys eat. He'd been eating mainly those energy bars, and he was so famished for fresh fruits and vegetables that he consumed an entire fresh fruit plate as an appetizer. Then he polished off a large roast beef and mashed potato dinner with all the trimmings. After that he accepted second and third helpings with a sheepish grin. He had the ability to make sure that we knew that he appreciated all that we did for him.

After he finished eating everything Kay had, Andrew asked to sleep in her unheated back room in order not to acclimate himself to indoor temperatures. "The North Country Trail volunteers were so hospitable," he said, "that I could have spent almost every night inside, but I was afraid that it would make me soft. It would have been more like I was dating the trail than having a relationship with it."

The next morning, after another massive meal, Stan Kujawa took Andrew up to his next trailhead on the family snowmobile. Both he and Kay were impressed that such "an amiable, spirited young man" kept traveling through winter to accomplish his goals "full speed ahead."

That was also the reaction on January 30 of Kirt Stage-Harvey of the NCT's Hiawatha Shore-to-Shore Chapter. He and his wife hosted Andrew for one night in St. Ignace, Michigan. As their visitor began his winter traverse of Michigan's Upper Peninsula, Kirt was beside himself with happiness. "I had the pleasure to hike that brief section with Andy through our Straits State Park while carrying my toddler daughter Sophia," he said. "A few days later, I arranged for Andy to stay in the cabin of one of our members near the mouth of the Tahquamenon River. I also sent him a note to be picked up at the Paradise Post Office to encourage him as he neared the half-way mileage mark of his hike." Kirt remembers that Andrew's clothing was so lightweight that he either had to keep moving to generate heat or be in his sleeping bag. "Andy said that he'd figured out how to pee while moving—but not always successfully!"

In retrospect, it is obvious that the NCT volunteers, in passing their visitor along from one family to the next, helped to give their own trail-maintaining labors an added dimension. Their experience is a reminder that a trail is just as much composed of people as it is of tread, signs, and stiles. Andrew's expedition became a journey of discovery for so many volunteers that it galvanized interest all along the little-used trail. Kay Kujawa told me:

> We were so fascinated by Andy's adventure that we not only continued to follow his progress westward but also visited Forillon Park in Quebec to experience the Atlantic Ocean cliffs where he'd begun his 7,700-mile march. To sum it all up, sure, we helped him a little bit when he was in our area, but he renewed in us the faith that our young people can not only be exemplary models for each other but for all of us regardless of age.

Volunteers and hikers will be talking about Andrew's eleven-month Sea-to-Sea trek for years to come. People who met him along the way will continue to repeat the story until his already sizeable achievement assumes Paul Bunyan proportions.

WALKING, SEEMINGLY the simplest of activities, is surprisingly multifaceted. It offers us as much pleasure as we have wit to enjoy. Dig as deeply as we can, and there is always more room for greater enjoyment and appreciation.

I am deeply grateful to the people who helped *me* when I was a novice hiker. Legendary trails activist Jeannette Fitzwilliams (1913–2010), a World War II RAF veteran, took me on my first overnight campout with the Potomac Appalachian Trail Club. As I mentioned earlier, Paris Walters was a constant source of encouragement. They and others inspired me when I sought not only places to go but someone to be.

I began this chapter with the idea that mentoring takes time because it is primarily about caring. So I want to end now with an example of what I meant. Recently I asked Andrew Skurka's mother to explain her role in her son's grand C2C adventure. She replied:

At first I was not in favor of Andy's C2C hike because I feared for his safety. Once I realized that he would proceed with it no matter what I thought, I focused on increasing his chance of survival. I really did not see my role as much different than that of the parent who attends every game or sends letters every day of camp. Parents who are involved with their kids have the opportunity to live with and through their children. Are we mentors? Of course. Do all parents mentor their children? I only wish that were true. I saw my role as being Andy's back-up crew. Knowing that he was actually picking up his packages gave me some assurance that he was doing okay. I could also see his progress and speak with many of the people that he met along the way. They e-mailed or called me, and I always responded. The e-mails and phone calls eased my fears, but also made Andy appear as more of an "all-American" kid. It helped both of us.

Mentoring our hiker provided insight into hiking that neither Bob nor I had prior to Andy's hike. Now our daughters hike with friends and we think nothing of it (though we won't trade our condo to go backpacking ourselves).

I never felt that what I did was so extraordinary. I grew up in a home where my parents were just as supportive of my endeavors as I have been with our kids. When I made two-week trips to Girl Scout camp, there were always mail and care packages from my mom and dad. I certainly expect my kids to do the same with their own children.

A large part of hiking's appeal is its focus on family, friends, and the environment. Andrew Skurka's long-distance hiking feats deserved their widespread national attention. However, too little recognition went to his relationship with his family. Karen Skurka is representative of all the many people who brought us each to the trailheads where we now find ourselves.

Along the PNT: The Purcell Mountains

I had wanted to quit it for years. I had a bear by the tail and couldn't let go. But I would have felt like a fool if someone else had gone in two more feet and struck it rich.
        Bill Tilly, hardrock miner, *River Pigs and Cayuses*, 1984

ON THE PACIFIC NORTHWEST TRAIL, I was surrounded by a lot more than scenery. As mentioned earlier, the trail's neighbors became the spice of my backwoods experience. In fact, for two decades I traveled with a tape recorder as often as with a backpack. I had no fixed base. Oral history paid poorly but the satisfaction was great. I followed wherever the trail of stories led. With no wife or children, I was free to roam at will, recruiting PNT volunteers and recording colorful stories. The volunteers and the old-timers were sometimes the same individuals. I was at home on the trail and in the past.

When I first explored the Purcell Mountains I heard of a hardrock miner named Bill Tilly. Just across Idaho's narrow Moyie Valley, on the fir-covered slopes of Hellroaring Mountain, the old Swede had spent fifty years blasting and tunneling. His trips out for logging jobs and for supplies became less and less frequent as his shafts multiplied and deepened. The odd part was that locals never heard of any pay dirt reaching market from the Tilly claims. One person recalled, "Once he told me that he was probably only 100 yards from the Mother Lode. I asked him what he would do when he reached it. 'Why, start tunneling in from another direction,' he said." Obviously Bill Tilly was a prime candidate for my oral history research.

On a rainy midsummer morning in 1977 I climbed high into the Purcell Mountains to search for the Tilly Mine. I thought I had hit pay dirt when I spotted a 5–foot-high shaft, but a hand-lettered sign warning of gas discouraged me from following it into the creepy depths of Hellroaring Mountain. So I squatted inside the low entrance to watch the steady downpour outside. Gloomy weather only added to the Tilly mystery. Who was he? I gave up my search that day and moved on to interview other people.

By chance, a year later, nearby at larger diggings, I happened upon a mackinawed man wearing a carbide helmet. "I am Bill Tilly," he said when I introduced myself.

Stanley meeting Livingstone could not have been happier. In fact, I was as psyched as the old Swede was phlegmatic. He searched his tidy cabin so long for a hearing-aid battery that I knew he never had any visitors. It was obvious that his only luxury was scenery. From a window above his sink, he could see 7,000-footers in Montana across the Moyie River Valley.

Though he spoke with no more grammatical quaintness than anyone else in Boundary County, Tilly's accent was as heavy as a pile of rubble. He was so short that he probably never needed to stoop in his tunnels.

Tilly said that he had immigrated from Sweden via Canada in 1928. After working for a few years in the woods around Priest Lake, he found himself jobless in the Great Depression. An old-time miner named Swen Anderson took him on as a helper, paying in mining stock. Bill planned to save enough money to return home to Sweden to buy a farm. Instead he became addicted to prospecting. "You walk around looking," he said, "for floats that break off from the vein and slide down the mountainside." Bill said that he had been working the Tilly Mine since 1947 and had dug 4,300 feet of tunnels by himself. "That's almost a mile!" I blurted. "Yeah," he replied calmly.

He definitely was a loner. In fact, he had sold his interest in one mine because the stockholders had not been able to agree on how to operate it. Being his own boss was very important to him. "Hell, it's working for yourself," he said. "You ain't going to do this kind of work for wages. It's being on your own. I'm the only prospector left in this part of the country, but there are a lot more mines here to be located. It's mostly luck."

FIVE YEARS LATER, in 1983, my friend Ted Hitzroth wanted me to introduce him to the legendary figure whom I'd been calling "the fragile old-timer who knows the Purcells better than anyone else." We feared the worst when we found the Tilly Mine's cabin boarded up, snowsheds broken, and portal collapsed. Maybe we had come too late.

Disappointed, we climbed toward the wooded summit of Bussard Mountain through a maze of bulldozer tracks. Suddenly we saw a short, determined man striding toward us. "It's Bill!" I cried. Tilly was unmistakable in his green mackinaw, red shirt, and black plastic eyeglasses. The rubber-booted prospector greeted me with his usual reserve. But before long he had us promising to join him for dinner at his trailer on Hellroaring Creek.

That evening inside his homemade caravan, we immediately knew that our man had learned his eating habits in logging camps. And we thought we were big eaters!

The stories, too, were oversized. I was particularly fascinated by his tales of Tom Moran, a prospector who had struck it rich in Helena's Last Chance Gulch, only to lose everything in a whorehouse betting scam. Moran's luck returned, though, when he bilked investors into grubstaking his claims. Because I wanted to locate the PNT there, Bill Tilly promised to show us the old-timer's cabin and trail. Ted and I bunked down in our tents, excited to see what the morning would bring.

We were less enthusiastic, though, before dawn, when Bill loudly chased away a porcupine who tried to eat his radiator hoses. The old prospector was as gruff with us as he was with the porky. "Up and at 'em!" he called.

The heat in his small trailer contrasted cheerily with the cold rain outside. As outdoorsmen always will, we discussed each other's gear. I liked Bill's low-tech approach. He said that a few years earlier he'd been so crippled with arthritis that he had had to stop working his tunnels. Wool had been his cure. Now he wore it even in summer. "Wool *filters the air* and keeps it from hurting your body," he said. I almost believed him.

The smell of freshly made griddle cakes finished the job of waking us up. But I despaired when I saw our host toss his first three creations out the door. Bill was such a perfectionist, as evidenced by his beautiful tunnels and woodwork, that only the best pancakes were good enough for guests.

He was like that in the woods, too. "He's not so *fragile*," laughed Ted as Bill, almost eighty, bounded ahead of us. The miner's cane was deceptive; he used it only to knock water off the brush. I readily believed his stories of Herculean winter hauls up the hogback, trail-less ridge on snowshoes.

Obviously Bill Tilly was a man in love with his world. Even if he found no gold he was not disappointed, he said. "Prospecting is always interesting because over the next hill there will be more mines to locate. Oh, I know I won't strike it the next day but I know it's ahead. And I always look forward to it." He led us through thick fog to see two new properties he had located along Tom Moran's old trail. Ted and I, no slouches with maps, definitely needed a guide for this one. Only Bill Tilly still knew where pack-string hooves had tamped the earth by that tree or had worn a groove in those flat rocks. We moved quickly on slick lichens and through dewy wildflowers. Frightened birds flew up as we passed. Bill seemed totally oblivious to the water that cascaded from his wool hat and mackinaw as he followed Tom Moran's arcane clues.

Our goal, the Kootenai Chief, Bill's newest prospect, was more mystical than anything I had dared to hope for. From afar it was a gash in the fog, a haunt of elves. Closer up, we saw that a wheelbarrow lay overturned in the earthen trench that Bill had dug two feet into the granite face. Our guide apologized for only having penetrated that far. In his prime, he said, he could have drilled a foot a day. He picked up a five-pound hammer and swung it underhand against a steel drill.

"Looks like hard work," I yelled.

"No, it ain't. Mucking is the hard work. Shoveling and wheeling it out. Drilling is easy when you get used to it. You start with a short drill and work up to using one four or five feet long. The most difficult thing is to get under the ground, to develop a portal. After that it's a lark! You get out of the weather, away from the mosquitoes."

I took the hammer and drill and scrunched down into the opening. Bill had already made an indentation in the vein's rotten rusty-brown quartz. I gave the drill a tentative whack, being careful not to bash my hand. One hundred dollars a ton, he'd said, for this unpromising stuff. I wondered how much lifting I would have to do to move a ton of it.

"I can bend over and swing like this all day and my back doesn't bother me a bit," he said. "But now I'm happy if I make six inches a day."

Bang! I hit the steel again. Wham! Suddenly I knew why Bill Tilly was nearly deaf. Clang! I'd had enough.

Bill planned to tunnel horizontally 100 feet along this tiny vein to Tom Moran's vertical vein of the 1930s. "Where two veins come together," he said, "you'll often find a jackpot." That had been the story, too, at the Tilly Mine's series of will-o'-the-wisps. Now, I learned, he'd recently sold the Tilly Mine for a measly $500. Five hundred dollars! My heart cried for him.

Bill Tilly would never see any "colors" other than the gold Sierra Club cup I gave him. I thought of the years he had spent at hard labor underground, his ears ringing with the deafening blows of his hammer.

"It's fun; it's a hobby," he said. "When Swen Anderson began prospecting, he asked Curly Jack how he liked it. Curly Jack told Swen, 'I'm seventy-two years old and I've been prospecting all my life and I never made a dollar. But if I had to live my life all over again, I'd do the same thing.'" Bill added, in case I hadn't understood, "And I feel the same way as Curly Jack."

"So why did you sell the Tilly Mine?" I asked.

"I had wanted to quit it for years," he said unexpectedly. "I had a bear by the tail and couldn't let go. But I would have felt like a fool if someone else had gone in two more feet and struck it rich."

I knew what he meant. Beginning in 1970, I spent decades locating and developing the Pacific Northwest Trail. For most of those years, I, too, had a bear by the tail. At least Bill Tilly knew when to let go.

"A Labor of Truly Obsessive Love"

I wrote two guidebooks. The first was published; the second was never finished. Both sold about the same number of copies. The truth is that guides are rarely well written, are soon out of date, and are not as useful as a good map or a route recommendation from a friend. I love to collect them—I have several guides to both the Pennine Way and the John Muir Trail, for example—but I wouldn't dream of using most of them.

"Crazy John" Manning, 2008
Yorkshire, England

MILE AFTER MILE, day after day, we hikers walk with an invisible companion whose writing colors the way we experience the trail. In fact, before we even arrive at the trailhead, our unseen escort often provides us with one of hiking's greatest pleasures: anticipation. But who is this person to whom we entrust ourselves? Do we really know anything about her or him?

As a lover of guidebooks, it was inevitable that I would eventually write multiple versions of the *Pacific Northwest Trail Guide*, "a labor of truly obsessive love" that compressed 1,200 miles into four hundred dense pages of technical writing. After Andrew Skurka used it during several PNT thru-hikes, he called it a "treasure hunt" because it seemed to describe less a trail than a series of arcane clues. For me personally, however, the emotional significance of my several editions was that they contained less a set of directions than a collection of between-the-lines memories.

LONG-DISTANCE PATHWAYS depend on public support for their continued upkeep and protection. If there are no users, eventually there will be no trail. An attractive guidebook is a kind of sales pitch to people who are looking for their next outing or vacation.

Nothing can build public support faster than a well-thought-out guide.

I designed my PNT guidebook to describe both a Practical Route that hikers could hike right away and an Ideal Route that future PNT trailbuilders would construct. In short, I wrote my guidebook to help conjure the Pacific Northwest Trail into being.

Long-distance trails are always evolving; some of the changes are not in backpackers' best interests. Having hiked many poorly located trails, I envisioned the PNT's Ideal Route as a future safeguard against ill-advised official routing decisions. For instance, I knew that eventually officials would want Section X to go down such and such a drainage because that route would require less labor to maintain than a more scenic alternate. I realized that such folly would be difficult to thwart, but as a long-distance hiker myself, I was determined to showcase each section's beauty. I wrote the PNT guidebook to sell that vision to as many people as possible.

Other guidebook writers have their own agendas. For instance, as I will describe a bit later, Jeff Schaffer of PCT fame wrote his guides to convey the wonders of geology. Harvey Manning, Puget Sound's outdoor guru, was totally obsessed with preserving endangered wilderness areas. I wish that more authors would convey not only trail data but also personal passions.

GUIDES COME IN several flavors such as data books, annotated maps, various forms of Internet postings, and full-featured guidebooks. Some are anonymously written under the aegis of a non-profit group, as in the case of the Appalachian Trail Conservancy's guides. Or an author such as the redoubtable Jeffrey Schaffer may create a commercial product such as his Wilderness Press three-volume series about the Pacific Crest Trail. A less-formal approach is that a wannabe author simply researches his or her favorite trail and (a) posts the information on a Web site or (b) self-publishes it. A popular example of the latter is *Yogi's PCT Handbook*.

In my humble opinion, guidebook writers must (1) present accurate, well-organized information and (2) convey their deep immersion in the subject. There is no substitute for personal experience out "where the boot hits the duff" (as Harvey Manning used to say). Lazy research and sloppy editing will be apparent to the hiker and to the reviewer. Poor writing may well create a bad impression of the trail itself. There is always room for a felicitous phrase or an apt metaphor that will serve to plant seeds of interest. We authors are like matchmakers who try to create a romance between readers and trails. To create a hiking guide is a high form of public service. To read one is to absorb the wisdom and/or quirks of a particular hiker.

The following two guidebook authors were among the most successful and memorable of the past fifty years.

JEFFREY SCHAFFER (1943–) wrote most of the Pacific Crest Trail's monumental, three-volume, 1,046-page guide. For almost four decades he was the ultimate authority for PCT information. Jeff's system of dividing the trail into letter sections is universally accepted by everyone from Campo, California, to Manning Park, British Columbia. For thru-hikers, Jeff was the best-known unknown person in the backcountry. For me, he was primarily a climber who got into PCT guidebook writing because of his deep-seated competitive streak. Recently he told me:

> *One day in 1972 I saw a Wilderness Press High Sierra hiking guide by Ron Felser in a bookstore window in Berkeley. Well, I was a better student at Cal than he was (and a better climber), so I figured I could write a better guidebook, even though I hated hiking guides because back then their minimal text and error-prone maps were pathetic.*

Jeff's idiosyncrasy was that his fascination with geology colored his route descriptions. That was already apparent in 1974 in his original Oregon-Washington guide. Many backcountry hikers, trying merely to decide whether to turn right or left, reacted angrily to distracting information such as the following:

Mt. Jefferson's Forked Butte was subsequently breached by outpourings of fluid basaltic andesite that flowed east down the glaciated Jefferson Creek and Cabot Creek canyons. A smaller cone with a crater lake, north of us, also erupted about this time, but it was aborted by nature before any flows poured forth. To its north stands the flat Table, and between it and the ridge of Cathedral Rocks is a large, deep, enigmatic depression that may represent a collapsed flow. Time, which allowed nature to sculpt this surrealistic art work, now forces us to press onward.

Press onward indeed! Of course, I admire Jeff for having had the gumption during the early 1970s to write the definitive PCT guidebook. But I am even more impressed that he attempted in the 1990s to revolutionize our geologic understanding of the High Sierra with his own revisionist reassessment of late Cenozoic mountain building. It makes me proud to think that a ridgerunning PCT hiker could possibly redefine how we see our beloved backcountry.

I am less pleased with Jeff's recent news that his much-valued guidebook will soon become extinct. In fact, Jeff predicts that publisher-produced, traditional guidebooks will soon be replaced by easily-upgradable electronic media. Already the U. S. Forest Service, Tony Nitz, Jonathan Ley, and others have created topographic maps of various long-distance trails that provide enough information to enable a hiker to navigate well-marked sections *without* a traditional guidebook. Jeff says, "Perhaps in the near future, all information will be available for free on the Internet. But I feel very content with my field work and with the books I produced from my maps and notes. There is great satisfaction in doing very good work."

That was well said. Change is inevitable, but we guidebook writers want to feel that we did the best that we could with what was available to us.

IF JEFF IS CORRECT that hard-copy guides are obsolete, then I might as well make a confession. Though I love daydreaming over guidebooks, I am usually equally fascinated by their authors' eccentricities. That's why I feel so lucky to have had the pleasure of knowing the most colorful guidebook writer of them all: HARVEY MANNING (1925–2006).

Even back in 1971 the imprimatur "Harvey Manning and Ira Spring" was the gold standard by which all other Pacific Northwest guidebooks were judged. Harvey wrote; Ira photographed. Born in Seattle, the former came of age in the Boy Scouts, then graduated to climbing with the Seattle Mountaineers. He observed at first hand the loggers' and miners' postwar assault on the region's mountains. Industry's rapaciousness offended him so much that he fought back with innumerable books designed to entice people to help preserve the threatened wilds. A Manning/Spring book was always as much about conservation as it was about telling you where to hike. Harvey used to say, "Anybody who is competent in English can put out a guidebook." In the same way that Jeff Schaffer used his guides to teach natural history, Harvey Manning's goal was to preach an environmental "call to arms." As a result, legions of hikers scurried into the hills toting numerous iterations of *100 Hikes in Western Washington* and *Footsore Around Puget Sound*. By today's standards, the books' black-and-white, planimetric, contour-free, sketch maps were substandard. GPS was

not in Harvey's vocabulary. But his and Ira's success spawned a publishing company, Mountaineers Books, and two generations of Nature lovers.

Harvey Manning's outsized persona was exceptionally blessed with personality tics. Anti-computer Luddite that he was, he used to tease me with statements such as, "What's a URL? No, don't tell me. It's probably one of these new diseases that are thinning the herd."

Though I hiked with Harvey only rarely, I corresponded with him from 1971 to 2005, first as a greenhorn East Coast interloper in his beloved Cascades and later as a controversial trail developer. Now, in rereading three decades' worth of letters, I appreciate more than ever his initial support for my pie-in-the-sky, wild-eyed attempt to construct a 1,200-mile east-west trail. Though he already had many conservation victories behind him, he never talked down to young me. In fact, his early 1970s encouragement was probably the main thing that kept me going.

> *Dear Ron,*
> *This'll be quick, since I'm just in and soon to go out again.*
> *Only time enough to catch up on crucial correspondence.*
> *We had eleven glorious days hiking the Olympic Wilderness*
> *Beaches, and before that it was eight days alone up the*
> *Stehekin, prowling the snowy forests, looking up at the*
> *icy peaks. Where next? Damn if I know, the snow still so*
> *deep and low. And rivers high and wild. Maybe the eastern*
> *Pasayten.*
> *As we ramble the hills and beaches, poor but happy, we*
> *think of you.*
> *Best,*
> *Harvey*

Beyond that, there was also his outspokenness and love of local history. With his bushy beard, unkempt clothes, and antiquated equipment he often resembled a troll or a backcountry Santa. I remember standing in line with him at a ranger station to obtain hiking permits. Some hikers ahead of us asked the seasonal know-nothing about a particular trail. Her ignorance prompted Harvey to erupt with a veritable Mt. St. Helens of information. Just for fun I told the hikers who he was, only to be then pushed aside as if I were accompanying a backwoods rock star.

Harvey once described himself to me as a "dependable technical writer." That was true as far as it went. But his "personal narrative," *Walking The Beach To Bellingham*, gives the real flavor of the man. It sings with memories of his large extended family as well as with rants about the destruction of forest, soil, and habitat.

I feel fortunate that e-mail didn't exist in 1971 when I began corresponding with Harvey, and I am thankful that he never abandoned his typewriter. Otherwise I wouldn't be able now to enjoy his excitement (in a stack of letters) about his "recent" hikes and be touched by his hopes for future ones. I love reading about his battles with some of Seattle's prickliest conservationists such as the "Earth Mother" whom he described as, "a single mosquito I fought all of a long night." Harvey, in alluding to his own "reputation as a controversialist," said that "Frequently in the new little good-thinking groups there are nice, reasonable people who don't want to make trouble and who are afraid of getting hooked up with mad-dog radicals." In the 1970s, I was less interested in his mad dog, radical side than in what I took to be our genuine friendship. For instance, I felt grateful during a short hospital stay in 1973 when Harvey wrote, "*Foot* operation! Are you okay? Worse things could happen to a gigolo, but for a hiker this is about the worst."

Harvey's bitterness in his last years was very sad. His letters no longer mentioned his eager anticipation to go hiking; sidelined by infirmity, he was off the trail in fact and in spirit. He wrote to me that the Crest Trail was a "fraud" and that the Rybackers were ruining the backcountry with their "Wreckreation." How, I wondered, could he still be angry at Eric Ryback and other "end-to-end automatons and stunters"? Why hadn't he mellowed about the Pacific Crest Trail's having been surveyed "by engineering college dropouts who didn't know it snowed in the Cascades but did know how to spend money for dynamite"?

He was angry at me, too. "The ludicrous monstrosities done in the Cascades [by the PCT engineers] were directly responsible for the instant antagonism your PNT encountered," he wrote. "Such supporters as you had then have swung away now, in the era of Industrial Wreckreation ... Look at it this way: you and your guidebook have earned a place on the shelf of the immortals beside *The High Adventure of Eric Ryback*."

There was worse. In 2003, he broke off his fifty-year friendship and collaboration with Ira Spring over a dispute about the title of their latest guidebook. In Seattle, where the public still took hiking seriously, the Manning vs. Spring dust-up played out in the press. Harvey explained it to me as "a profound difference in philosophy." My reaction was that friendship is the supreme philosophy and that Harvey was foolish to publicly alienate someone who had stood by him for so long.

Harvey's books contained in-your-face rants against such deviltries as horses, dogs, and bicycles on trails. In his last years, his diatribes against long-distance hikers and long-distance trails crossed the line beyond colorful cantankerousness to promoting a wrongheaded, purist view of environmentalism. Yet he had also been instrumental in creating such gems as the Mountains-to-Sound Greenway, the Issaquah Alps, the Alpine Lakes Wilderness, the Cougar Mountain Regional Park, and most of all, the North Cascades National Park. He was a complex person whom I never stopped admiring despite deep-seated disagreements. In late 2000, he typed out an *apologia pro sua vita* on his old typewriter and sent it to me in what I now realize was a wistful good-bye:

Ai-yee Ron!
I've cast the old world off to go it alone. I did my best but
it's incorrigible, and we'll just have to sit back and await the

Asteroid, and plan to get a running start with the Day of the
Sludgeworm.

    It's not just the large world that's fracturing. The little
world of environmentalism has got too big for its britches,
and as goes the society when it gets a bit of tin in the pocket,
is swarming up the landscape with ballooning egos.

    There was a time when we all looked up to titans. But the
mightiest of them was toppled by the Lilliputians years ago.
Me, I've just quietly gone away, and will stay away until
the Second Coming, which will be ridin' an Asteroid, as is
promised in Leviathan V: 32.116.

    Keep the aspidistra flying,
    Harvey

Despite whining about Eric Ryback's promotion of long-distance trails, Harvey Manning himself publicized the Northwest backcountry more than any other writer of his time. In the process, over more than four decades, he lived a maximum-hiking lifestyle beyond that of anyone I've ever known. After the very wet summer of 1975, he wrote me on September 13, two weeks after the sun finally reappeared, that:

The appetite is as wild as ever now, and lest not all the
summer escape me, I'm off for four days—first to Mt. Baker
to see the steaming volcano, then wherever seems fit. If we
have the kind of September we had last year, and October
(both terrific), the mountain season has a full month to go.
Best not to take chances ... But damn, you can't let [the sun]
go on and on [without getting out to hike].

Harvey believed in hiking as often as humanly possible. And that's the way that I choose to remember America's most prolific guidebook writer: eager to hit the trail and excited to write about it.

WE ARE ENJOYING a glorious period of new trail development. But even our old established trails sometimes benefit from the invention of new ways of describing them. For instance, Jackie "Yogi" McDonnell supplemented Jeff Schaffer's encyclopedic PCT volumes with her excellent *Yogi's PCT Handbook*. Advertised as a "planning and hiking resource," it was "written by hikers for hikers" in the sense that she used contributions from many people to assemble it. Another example is David "Awol" Miller's *The A.T. Guide*. In 2010, he combined detailed on-trail information with elevation profiles, GPS waypoints, town data, etc. in a compact, highly usable format. I wish that every long trail could benefit from his ingenuity.

Jackie McDonnell and David Miller had clever ideas and ran with them. And, speaking of inventive approaches, I wish that more guidebook authors would critique the design of the worst trails they encounter. Many trails are poorly maintained, ill routed, or badly constructed. Guidebooks, blogs, articles, and Web sites should highlight such failings and offer attractive solutions. I want the public to know that most Western trails were designed in the 1920s and 1930s for administrative, emergency, livestock, and fire-suppression purposes and that the trails' locations were definitely not chosen to optimize twenty-first-century recreational-hiking needs. Guidebook writers should explain that what was appropriate for strings of pack mules in 1935 is not necessarily adequate for today's view-seeking backpackers (even though we sometimes feel like beasts of burden).

My frustration with traditional guidebooks is that I love them for nostalgic reasons even as I realize that they sometimes don't give me the information that I want in the format that I need. For instance, if I day hike on the PCT, I need more information about loop trails than a thru-hiker would require. And if I love clams (as I surely do), I will want as much information as possible about nearby clam shacks.

Of course, projected sales loom large in publishers' marketing decisions. And there has been a tendency to shy away from backcountry, multi-day guides because of a perceived shift in the public's preference for short, less-strenuous outings. Carried to its logical extreme this trend would leave adventurous hikers in the lurch if it were not for certain countervailing forces such as GPS and the Internet. The future is surely in small electronic devices, though I predict that they will never entirely supplant hard-copy guidebooks and maps.

As I said before, we authors are like matchmakers who try to create a romance between readers and trails. In 2009, I developed a serious lust for the newly designated New England National Scenic Trail. So I rushed out, all atwitter, to order its guides for Connecticut and Massachusetts. When I finally held them in my hands I felt the old excitement radiate from every page. *The New England Trail*, I thought. *Let me at it ...*

"Willful and Eccentric"

These trail maintainers were all possessed of firm
convictions; were unafraid to make decisions and assume
full responsibility for getting the job done; were terribly hard
workers themselves and not always effective delegators of
work to others; were sometimes inclined to be contemptuous
of those less dedicated than they; and were apt to believe
that there was one right way to fix a trail (theirs).
Guy and Laura Waterman, *Forest and Crag*, 1989

SOME OF MY ALL-TIME favorite people devoted their lives to passionate involvement with trails. Unpaid, they found their calling out of sheer enthusiasm. Their energy was so contagious that they influenced me—just as I hope to influence future volunteers now.

Here are a few examples.

DURING THE EARLY YEARS of the PNT, its neighbors often asked me to name my favorite part of its 1,200-mile route. Naturally, devious rascal that I am, I always lavished praise on their own sections. However, I did truly love northeast Washington's beautiful Pend Oreille County. The problem was that it was so sparsely populated and economically depressed that I never could find any local volunteers until twenty-four-year-old Bob Mathews (1953–1984) sent in membership dues and an offer to help. Because even a smidgen of interest quickly got my attention, I soon visited him at "Mathews Acres" within sight of the Trail's Hooknose-Abercrombie ridge route.

1978 was one of America's recurring periods of popular infatuation with rural living. So it was no surprise that the friendly, dark-haired back-to-the-lander, fearing "severe economic and political times," boasted that *he* would soon be almost completely self-sufficient. "We want to build a fish pond up here in the clearing so we have plenty of protein available. We'll run a couple of head of cattle and put in an acre vegetable garden and build a greenhouse. Some things do well here such as comfrey—which is real big on our list." Having grown up in the country myself, I was immune to such agrarian urges. Comfrey, for instance, despite its cult status, did nothing for me. However, I sympathized with Bob's search for peace and quiet. Hadn't I been a seeker myself on the Pacific Northwest Trail? So I listened attentively when he said, "Five days a week I work in the constant noise of the cement factory in Metaline Falls. And it's really a relief to come up here where there's no noise except for the birds singing. This is like a little Eden. There's no hassle: just paradise."

A year after that encounter, during my next circuit-riding tour, Bob and I organized Pend Oreille County's first PNT meeting. We had a good turnout, and afterward I met his new bride, Debbie. She had been one of 133 respondents to his *Mother Earth News* personals ad.

Young Christian male in need of intelligent, mature woman 18-22 years old to help me work with and enjoy the plants and animals and bees on my small homestead in the Selkirk Mountains in northeastern Washington.

With successful marketing like that I was certain that Bob Mathews would become a dynamic PNT leader. However, I never heard from him again.

Eventually someone told me that Bob had "moved on to other interests." I thought no more about him until July 1984, when I wanted to include his personal story in one of my books. I telephoned Debbie, who informed me that her husband was "away on business." Within a few months he was dead.

Bob Mathews died such an incredibly violent death that to this day I scarcely believe what happened. The facts are clear, however. On the run from the FBI after a string of daring felonies, Bob holed up on Whidbey Island, not far from the PNT at Smugglers

Cove. After a thirty-six-hour standoff and shootout, he perished when agents incinerated his hideout with M-79 Starburst flares. The news came as a total shock. I had no idea that Bob had led a secret life as Führer of a band of domestic terrorists known as the Silent Brotherhood. He and his band of assassins and bank robbers were out to transform the Pacific Northwest into a racist "white bastion." That was quite a switch from growing comfrey.

Six years earlier I had been certain that Bob was prime volunteer material. However, his *Mother Earth News* jargon had disguised the fact that he was a high school dropout awash in a toxic mix of John Birch and Neo-Nazi hatred. My mistake was understandable. Without volunteers the PNT would be toast. I was so focused on recruiting that I unwittingly befriended one of America's most dangerous terrorists.

Years later I learned that Bob first attempted to finance his racist revolution with a successful bid for a *trail maintenance* contract. When that work proved too physically demanding he led his gang on a much easier counterfeiting and robbery spree. Beginning with a $369 stickup at a Spokane porn shop, Bob's career culminated with a $3.6 million Brinks armored-car heist. Maybe *I* should give that a try the next time that I tire of trail maintenance.

A HALF CENTURY after my family went into exile in Delaware after the collapse of the New England textile industry, I fetched up near Concord, Massachusetts, within fifty miles of my birthplace. My partner, Christine "Tine" Hartmann, got a job as a Veterans Administration researcher, and I found work as a docent at the Old Manse, the farm where on April 19, 1775, Minutemen and British Regulars had fought the first pitched battle of the American Revolution.

> *By the rude bridge that arched the flood,*
> *Their flag to April's breeze unfurled,*
> *Here once the embattled farmers stood,*
> *And fired the shot heard round the world.*

In 1836 when this Concord Hymn was published by Ralph Waldo Emerson, the town sheltered an astonishing collection of literary celebs. I often sensed their presence almost two centuries later at the Old Manse. Defying time, Nathaniel and Sophia Hawthorne's graffiti still adorned some of its windows. Corn, beans, and squash flourished in the garden planted by Henry David Thoreau. He, the Hawthornes, the Alcotts, and many other Concordians flavored the town with their outsized personas, particularly that of Ralph Waldo Emerson.

Waldo, as he was called, wrote his seminal treatise *Nature* in the Manse's upstairs study, where the room's bucolic view of the Concord River contributed to the birth of Transcendentalism. However, for me Waldo was simply the town's practical-minded civic booster. Not only did he write the Concord Hymn (quoted above) to commemorate the famous North Bridge battle but he also helped develop and dedicate the Sleepy Hollow Cemetery (where he now rests). He was the indispensable man, the Sage of Concord.

He supposedly said, "Do not go where the path may lead; go instead where there is no path and leave a trail." I believe that if he were alive today, he would surely love the 220-mile New England Trail (NET), since for almost a century its leaders have fit the very definition of Emersonian self-reliance. I am thinking especially of librarian Frederick Wilkinson Kilbourne (1872-1965). His original Trap Rock Trail (built from 1916 to 1919) became the model for several trails that were constructed by hard-charging Connecticut Yankees during the 1930s. I am less interested here in the details of their routes than in their own quirks: "headstrong, self-reliant, geographically dispersed, not easily led." My favorite example was a retired General Motors patent attorney named Romeyn Spare, the creator of the Tunxis Trail. It was said of him that he had a one-track mind. "He ate, slept, and dreamed trails."

[I]n prewar titans such as Heermance, Anderson, and Spare all the elements of the genre are there: the single-minded

devotion to good trail work, the fierce dedication, the
volcanic energy, the unabashed pride, often tinged with
disdain for those less dedicated, the marvelous decades-long
record of achievement. Spare was known as Baron von
Tunxis, a title expressive of the feudal sway over their trails
that these men exercised.

Professor Walter M. Banfield (1902–1998) was another classic example of the breed. During the 1950s he extrapolated Kilbourne's north-south Connecticut work up through Massachusetts to New Hampshire. The authoritative *Forest and Crag* described the "cantankerous and opinionated" biologist as "the willful and eccentric czar of the Metacomet-Monadnock and other Massachusetts trails, whose fiery leadership and lethal swing of swizzle stick and brush hook continued with undiminished force into his upper eighties."

By the time that Prof. Banfield died, his Metacomet-Monadnock Trail was a thoroughly marked, revered resource. Its future, however, looked bleak. Rapid economic development threatened so many sections that Congressman John Olver became concerned. The Mattabesett-Monadnock Trail had enabled him to experience the natural beauty of his district but he feared that "without permanent easements" it might disappear. Very few members of Congress are trained naturalists, but Olver's intense personal interest in the natural world was a major factor in 2009 in Congress's designating the NET as a national scenic trail. Recently, in his understated, Yankee way, he summed up his philosophy.

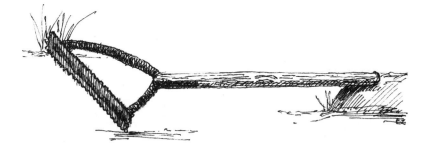

"People would be better off," he told me, "if they got out and smelled the flowers a little bit."

I ARRIVED IN GUILFORD, Connecticut, on National Trails Day 2009 to thru-hike John Olver's new creation. My companion, Bart Smith, had just completed a thru-hike of the 900-mile Arizona Trail and was in such superb shape that at first I worried about being able to keep up. Worried, that is, until I noticed that he was lugging around enough Nikon camera gear to slow down an elephant.

Before beginning our trek north, we fell under the tutelage of a handsome sixty-six-year-old volunteer named Paul Mei (1937 -). The former wine salesman was well into his second career as a trail development hotshot with the Connecticut Forest and Park Association. His primary goal was to link Long Island Sound to the existing Mattabesett Trail via a new, 15-mile connector that he called the Menukatuck Trail (after Guilford's original inhabitants). Over the course of several days, Paul introduced us to at least half of Guilford's residents. Many of them said they were proud that the town and its land trust had (over many decades) preserved about five thousand acres. Paul's challenge was to thread his new route through some of that land as well as past, over, and/or by a major rail line, an Interstate, and a tidal estuary. He and the other planners also had to please Guilford's selectmen, who wanted the new Menukatuck section to (1) use their Amtrak depot's pedestrian bridge, (2) pass the oldest stone house in New England, and (3) include the town green, formerly the site of a colonial graveyard and a cattle pasture.

Bart and I spent two days following our guide through Guilford's woodlots, cemeteries, historic homes, and salt marshes in search of possible NET routes. Paul's encyclopedic knowledge of properties and personalities was constantly on display. I thought of him as the spiritual heir of earlier trails leaders such as Baron von Tunxis, except that Paul was a master at building community support. As his colleague Heather Allore told me, "Paul is always reaching out to people, whether it be Cub Scouts or retirees. His cheerfulness is irresistible in getting them to build and maintain Guilford's extensive trail system. Paul is our Great Outdoors Gentleman Gem. Without him we would not have the NET's connection from Long Island Sound north through our historic district."

DESPITE ITS PRIOR HISTORY as the 3-M Trail, the NET was much less developed than Bart and I had expected. Camping facilities were almost nonexistent. In fact, the Connecticut Forest and Park Association actually prohibited overnight camping on the predominantly privately owned trail. That policy was about as welcome to us thrus as a requirement to load our packs with rocks. "They can't really expect us to find a motel every night?" said Bart. "Wanna bet?" I replied. "Notice that they haven't told us where the motels are or how to walk there from the trailheads."

Of course, Bart and I were seasonal experts at slipping off into the brush at sundown to hole up for the night. At the end of our first soggy day north of Guilford, we were about to do exactly that when we were pleasantly surprised to find an unofficial homemade shelter belonging to local quarry mechanic David Peters. Bart and I were delighted to discover that he loved the Appalachian Trail so much that he'd built a double Adirondack shelter on his property, just ten feet from the NET. "I do a lot of hiking," he said, "and I wanted to be able to unwind and relax here after work."

Trail magic is a delight whenever it materializes. Cattails Shelter's classic three-sided Adirondack shape was as organic as a forest mushroom. It popped into our lives just when lightning and thunder tried to blow us out of the woods. Despite Nature's pyrotechnics, we slept soundly thanks to David's trail-angel hospitality.

June 2009 in Connecticut was unusually rainy—not that we Puget Sounders were discouraged by the mists, downpours, and fogs that accompanied us north. Every oak or nut tree leaf was a waterfall. Each day the Nutmeg State surprised us with its wild beauty. Even the geology seemed somehow familiar. We often hiked rocky ridges that reminded us of Washington state's ancient lava flows. But instead of "basalt," Connecticut locals used the odd term "trap rock." Reddish, unpromising trap rock was the basis of two of the NET's leading industries: quarries and shooting ranges. The former pocked the rolling landscape with craters, and the latter startled us each time that large- and small-bore weapons let loose with volleys of lead.

Sloshing northward, we alternated long valley walks with cliff-top panoramas. One afternoon, after a foggy trek down from the heights of Lamentation Mountain, we followed the trail past a tire- and trash-filled forest whose owner had reportedly wanted to turn the land into an ORV "park." Thwarted by his upscale neighbors, he had created an unholy mess, perhaps to spite them. Truly America is a land of extremes, and hikers see it all. Not far away we came to a mansion of such overblown proportions that we stopped to gape. The guard at the gate told us that the place had first belonged to a Wall Street criminal, second to boxer "Iron Mike" Tyson, and third to rap artist 50 Cent, whose credo was summed up in "Get Rich or Die Trying." So I was saddened when a local person told us (incorrecly) that hard times had forced the gazillionaire rapper to unload his Gatsby-like estate.

"Don't you think this mansion would make a fabulous National Trails Center?" I asked Bart. "What could be better than this location right on the New England National Scenic Trail?"

"Why, do you think 50 Cent is a hiker?" he asked.

"Of course, he is," I lied. "And he *deserves* a trail name."

"Such as?" said Bart. "*50 Cent* already sounds like a trail name."

"It's not accurate, though," I said. "How about if we call him Two Bits or Bad Penny?"

"Aren't you forgetting something?" laughed Bart.

"What?"

"He has a reputation for violence and he can give you a trail name, too. I already know what it will be."

"What?"

"T.O.S."

"Meaning?" I asked.

"It's the title of one of his raps: 'Terminate On Sight'."

AT THE TIME of our hike in 2009, I did not like the idea that management of the New England Trail was going to reside in a Stewardship Council made up of representatives of all the NET's interest groups. I feared that since everyone would have veto power nothing would ever get done. Also, I was frustrated that the NET's enabling legislation had specified that the trail's northern terminus would be the New Hampshire state line. I'd been thinking for years about linking the Connecticut and Massachusetts NET with the Appalachian Trail (in New Hampshire) and the Trans Canada Trail (in Quebec). I am happy to report now that the hard work and infectious enthusiasm of the NET's very capable volunteers have mostly allayed my fears.

Bart was much more practical than I was. Instead of daydreaming about trail policy he somehow managed to find an unopened bottle of Bud in a ditch. His resulting smile was the sunniest thing I had seen all summer. Drinking that beer renewed his good spirits after days of rain.

In Massachusetts we encountered Pat Fletcher (1942–), the Bay State's equivalent of Connecticut's Paul Mei. Pat, like Paul, had come to trail development late in life. After working as a clerk on five different railroads, he retired from CSX, and became chair of the AMC's Berkshire Chapter Trail Committee.

I hiked the entire Metacomet Trail in 1989. Two years later I was shanghaied into being trails chair at an AMC work party. At that time our Metacomet Trail was still what we called a "guerilla trail." Professor Banfield had sometimes gotten handshake agreements for it and sometimes he hadn't. But when I took over in 1991 I wasn't comfortable with locating trail without asking permission from landowners. I knew that those guerilla tactics often come back to bite you in the butt.

When Bart and I met him in 2009, Pat spoke excitedly about protecting the NET for his four grandchildren. I recognized that like all great trail stewards, he felt an emotional stake in his trail's future. This was confirmed later when I met the Appalachian Mountain Club's Deborah Levine who told me of his long-time devotion.

> *Whether he is at meetings or out in the woods maintaining and rerouting, he gives countless hours of his time and energy. His selfless dedication extends from every detail of the trail's legislation and land management to the intricacies of the outhouses and shelters he has constructed. He is an inspiration.*

Baron von Tunxis in the 1920s did not have to operate within Pat's twenty-first-century context of complicated partnerships, restless stakeholders, and abstruse regulations. To construct a trail the baron simply located a route, corralled husky volunteers, and (sometimes) arranged handshake easements. During the PNT's first two decades, I, too, sometimes operated like a would-be Daniel Boone. Nowadays with so much changed, I miss that fun almost more than I can say.

THERE MUST BE something about trail volunteering that attracts even a shy, retiring person such as myself. Actually "zealot" was the way famed mountaineer John Harlin described me in *Backpacker Magazine*:

> *The lanky, narrow-boned man at my side spies two hikers headed our way. Ron Strickland steps to the side of the trail and slips his pack from his shoulders. He calmly glides his hand into the pack's top pocket as if he's done this a thousand times. Out comes a yellow pamphlet, which Strickland flips in his fingers to expose the prominent title to the dayhikers.*

*By the time the middle-age couple reaches us, the
evangelist is ready, and my gaze has dropped to the dirt in
embarrassment. Looking earnest, helpful, and not to be
ignored, Strickland pipes up as the targets draw abreast.
"Did you know you're hiking along the Pacific Northwest
Trail?" he inquires.*

*"Why no," they respond, just a little startled by the
directness of the question, as well as by the proffered
brochure and business card. But they're intrigued, as it turns
out, and I watch with growing fascination while Strickland
proselytizes. The duo apparently owns a nearby restaurant,
so Strickland suggests that they offer discounted meals to
thru-hikers trekking the entire route from Montana to the
Pacific Ocean.*

"But how would we recognize such a hiker?" one asks.

*"Simple," says Strickland, pulling down his sock, "by their
tan lines."*

*By the time Strickland picks up his pack, the hikers have
been converted into loyal supporters of a trail they'd never
heard of until ten minutes earlier.*

When John Harlin described me as a "pulpit-pounding evangelist," he placed me squarely in the tradition of all the "willful
and eccentric" trail builders of the last hundred years. That's
fair enough, but our trails need construction and maintenance
volunteers whose satisfaction comes from work well done and
from camaraderie with like-minded indivduals.

I began this chapter with the story of my misplaced eagerness to
recruit back-to-the-lander Bob Mathews. His treasonous rampage
of robbery and assassination was a reminder of the craziness and
violence that all too often lurk just below society's surface. For
a while after that fiasco I was too chagrined to hustle for new
helpers. Luckily today I know for sure that a potential recruit is
waiting just around the next switchback. I've learned a hard lesson,

though. From now on I will always ask whether he or she has ever grown comfrey.

Ten Essentials

Out on the Crest Trail, there's a wind a-blowin', A mountain wind, blowin' 'way my cares. It's pushing me northward, that's where I'm a-goin', I'm bound for the border and I'll soon be there.
 Walkin' Jim Stoltz, "Out on the Crest Trail," 1996

HIKING HAS THE POTENTIAL to be so much more than just schlepping from Point A to Point B. There are many ways to enjoy it. For instance, some people like me invent new trails. Others help fellow hikers by becoming trail angels. Some good souls join trail clubs to carry on the work of maintenance and construction. As I have mentioned elsewhere, mentoring is an especially valuable way to pass on our love for the outdoors. People who do these unglamourous things rarely make the evening news, but they do finish most days with a feeling of genuine accomplishment.

As many hikers know, the phrase "ten essentials" refers to certain items that should be in everyone's pack. In this chapter, I will offer an analogous list of hiking activities and a roster of individuals who best personify them, exemplifying outstanding service to the trails community.

Trail Founder:
Jim Kern

LET'S BEGIN at the beginning. Someone had to initiate the long-distance trails that we enjoy today. True, Native Americans had extensive networks of pathways well before the arrival of Europeans. But our "national scenic trails," such as the Appalachian, Pacific Crest, and the Continental Divide, were invented for foot-powered recreation by specific individuals. Take, for instance, Long Trail founder James P. Taylor. In 1909, he proposed to make "the Vermont mountains play a large part in the life of the people" by developing a path, now 270 miles long, through the Green Mountains from Massachusetts to Quebec. To that end, he founded the Green Mountain Club, a model for all subsequent trail-maintaining, volunteer nonprofits.

Those trail-founding visionaries deserved more acclaim than they ever received. They contributed incalculable benefits to our national well-being, yet even Appalachian Trail founder, Benton MacKaye, went largely unrecognized by his fellow citizens.

James Kern (1935–) is another such hero. As a Miami realtor in the early 1960s, he fell in love with hiking after an Appalachian Trail section hike with his brother. Upon his return home he realized that his own state offered nothing comparable. So Jim founded the Florida Trail Association to recruit volunteers (annual dues were $1) to create a trail the length of the state. He kicked off the plan with a *Miami Herald* publicity hike from the wilds of Big Cypress to Highlands Hammock State Park. In 1966, he persuaded Ocala National Forest to permit him to start blazing what he called the Florida Trail. Despite that modest start, anyone wishing to thru-hike the FT today would be treated to a continuous 1,200-mile semi-tropical experience, all thanks to Jim's original leadership.

But that's not the full extent of his genius for institution building. In 1977, he became the founding president of the American Hiking Society. In 1990, he founded Big City Mountaineers to take disadvantaged city kids backpacking in adventurous places such as the Rockies. I could go on and on about Jim Kern's impressive contributions, but I want to emphasize instead that even in his seventies he has not lost his love of hiking. During the past few years, he hiked Nepal's Langtang Range, Pakistan's Hunza Valley, and various parts of Alaska. Recently he told me, "I still feel as excited about hiking as I did more than forty years ago when I organized the First Florida Trail hikes."

Git 'Er Done Trail Couple:
Bobby and Deb Koepplin

TO THRU-HIKE a long-distance trail is equivalent to running marathons day after day for months at a time. To develop a long-distance trail requires just as much stamina but spread out over a period that may extend for decades. Of the two, thru-hiking is much easier.

Sometimes people ask me about the skills necessary to become a trail developer. I respond that the ideal candidate would be a clone of Bobby and Deb Koepplin (1955–) of Valley City, North Dakota.

Trails are somewhat analogous to electrical power line rights-of-way. As manager of rural development for Cass County Electric Cooperative in southeast North Dakota, Bobby Koepplin has many years of experience planning and administering multi-million-dollar construction projects. He parlayed these skills into a spare time volunteer job as chairperson of the 63-mile Sheyenne River Valley National Scenic Byway. That led eventually to a second volunteer career in a series of high-level roles in the North Country Trail Association. As president from 2009 to 2011, he spearheaded extending the NCT westward from mid-North Dakota to Montana's Continental Divide Trail.

Bobby recalls, "I developed my passion for the North Country Trail after my wife Deb and I chose to make a positive difference in our community rather than just complain about things. We participate because we believe that every person has an obligation to give back to society."

Deb Koepplin met her husband at North Dakota State University when they were both nineteen. She says, "Looking back, even in college Bobby was already very involved in all kinds of organizations and worthy projects." Today Deb is both a banker and the president of the Sheyenne River Valley Chapter of the North Country Trail Association. As such she faces an uphill challenge in finding enough volunteers to complete the construction of the NCT's local segments. However, she thrives on working with people and being outdoors. "My involvement with the North Country Trail has given me the opportunity," she says, "to do both while introducing the community to America's finest trail."

Private-sector Innovator:
Craig Della Penna

CRAIG DELLA PENNA (1952–) is a go-get-'em realtor who lives and breathes former railroad corridors. During a twenty-year career he marketed rail freight and operated two of New England's largest and most successful railroad-owned trans-loading facilities. His passion for railroad history led to his writing three guidebooks about rail-trails and to his working for the Rails-To-Trails Conservancy (RTC) as their New England representative. He specialized in assisting communities where residents feared that a proposed rail-trail would bring criminals into their neighborhoods. After 2004, when RTC downsized his job, Craig and his wife Kathleen renovated a Civil War-era farmhouse and transformed it into Northampton's Maple Sugar Inn, located a mere 8 feet from the oldest municipally built rail-trail in southern New England. Craig continues to push for walking-biking solutions at the grassroots community level, where they are so desperately needed.

I wish that someone in every city would adopt Craig's clever methods, including buying and selling residential properties near rail-trails and other greenways. I am particularly impressed that he and a couple of friends set up a land-acquisition company called Central Highlands Conservancy (CHC) to track the sale of former railroad corridors. When such property became available—and was in danger of being sold off to adjacent landowners who would block public access—CHC stepped in, bought it, and asked a local land trust to repurchase it through a capital fund-raising campaign. Craig describes that process as being "akin to putting Humpty Dumpty together again."

CHC focuses on former railroad corridors that could become "part of a regional network and have the capability to provide an off-road connection between schools, downtown areas, city/ town services and recreation areas." The group's first project in 2007 sold 3.5 miles of corridor, including four large bridges, to a regional land trust. In 2008, they saved more than two more miles.

Craig also hosts an ongoing lecture series to teach communities not only *how* to build rail-trails but also *why* it is necessary to do so. He himself has presented more than a thousand such talks; I very much admire his dogged persistence. At public hearings in communities that are planning to build a rail-trail, he usually sits in the back of the room until the project's opponents have stopped foaming at the mouth about why the conversion of the derelict former railroad corridor would return the community to the Dark Ages. Then he speaks calmly about his real-life experience of living 8 feet from a rail-trail. He even offers opponents a complimentary weeknight (during the school year) stay at his bed and breakfast in Northampton. He explains that so many kids walk and bike to school on that rail-trail that it obviates the need to pay for two school buses. In fact, so many kids use the pathway in winter that the town now plows it to encourage even more use. "How many kids in your towns walk and bike to school?" he asks skeptics.

Many people are tempted to think of the private-enterprise system as something inexorably opposed to public-interest projects such as trails. However, Craig Della Penna has proved that the market can be manipulated very effectively to serve the needs of hikers.

Government Official:
Tom Gilbert

AT FIRST GLANCE, hiking might not seem like a promising avenue for paid employment, but actually there are definite possibilities for such a career. Tom Gilbert (1950–) was my favorite example. As National Park Service superintendent for both the Ice Age National Scenic Trail and the North Country National Scenic Trail, this diplomat dealt with all kinds of people including landowners, cranks, and congressmen—not necessarily in that order. Over many years I saw Tom groan with frustration at the bureaucracy. But more often I felt that if he weren't paid to develop the NCT, he would be out there doing it anyway as a volunteer.

That is currently the case with Bill Menke, who was Tom's right-hand man before retiring to work for the North Country Trail Association. Bill tells me that he still thinks of Tom Gilbert as the trail's institutional memory. "I can think of no one," Bill says, "who can so easily recite the many small-but-critical elements of the trail's legislation, rules, and regulations. Tom's retirement in 2011 left very big shoes for his successor to step into."

I remember sharing a dorm room with Tom at a trails conference and waking up at 3 a.m. only to find him doggedly finishing a report for the next day's meeting. He was like that about every aspect of completing the North Country Trail.

Long-distance trails take many long decades to develop, and it is a rare person who can sustain a high level of dedication over the course of a working lifetime. But Tom's devotion went beyond the nitty-gritty of easements and handicapped-access regs. As the NCT's institutional public face, Tom Gilbert was always quick to pay tribute to others for work in which he himself often played a large part. For any hiker considering government employment, he is an inspirational example of someone who gracefully combined trails idealism with devoted public service.

Hiking Buddy:
Ted Hitzroth

OFTEN I HIKE ALONE. But, for months at a time, I've also explored the backcountry with my buddy Ted Hitzroth (1957 –). He originally joined me in 1983 to draw maps for my first guidebook by completing a thru-hike of the entire route. He was young and crazy enough to take a chance on the PNT even though it was an unsigned, unblazed, pie-in-the-sky trail that had been universally written off for dead.

When we began our two-and-a-half-month trek at Glacier National Park in Montana, Ted and I were as odd a pair as Paris Walters and Earl Shaffer had been on the Cascade Crest Trail twenty-one years earlier. I loved to talk to everyone; Ted was the ultimate introvert. I was the disorganized large-scale dreamer; he was the nuts-and-bolts practical planner. Though my new buddy was fifteen years younger than I, he was more adept at reprovisioning us every five to twelve days from supply boxes mailed to ourselves c/o general delivery at local post offices. I was also thankful that he carried more than his share of our gear since I was recovering from an almost-fatal bicycle accident. Best of all, he was as eager as I was to cross the Rockies, Purcells, Selkirks, Cascades, and Olympics to reach the Pacific Ocean. His unfailing good humor was evident from the start.

A long trek or climb is a famously difficult crucible in which to get to know someone. Friends fight and spouses spar. Storms, bugs, injuries, hunger, thirst, and illness test people's tolerance. Ted and I, near-total strangers, stepped off the international boat at Goat Haunt in Glacier National Park June 17, bubbling over with big hopes and cheap champagne. We spent our first month slogging through rain and bushwhacking across compacted snow. After that, the sun baked us, and our gear malfunctioned. However, humor lightened our loads. To this day Ted still makes fun of the way I "yogied" a homestay from a nice lady we met near a county landfill during a downpour. "Oh, I guess we'll just go set up our tent in the dump," I said pitifully. Of course, I never let him forget the time we camped on wet new snow atop an exposed ridge and his doorstop-heavy boots froze so solidly that they were useless the next morning.

In bad times, we both knew enough to treasure small joys. One stormy afternoon, hiking cross-country west from Two Mouth Lakes, we finally emerged from a horrific tangle of alders. Everything was soaked, including our spirits. But to create a little cheer I pulled a wet but fairly pristine chocolate bar out of a secret stash and presented it to my buddy. The gratitude on his face was priceless.

During that summer of 1983, as we navigated from one obscure clue to the next, we became a backcountry team, able to complement each other's skills and personalities. Ted once described my age to someone in terms of tree rings. He observed, "Ron may have many rings, but they're very narrow rings." I always regarded him with that same degree of tolerant affection.

Ted claims that long ago on the PCT he discovered that there are two kinds of people: Oxydol People and thrus. "When I pulled out my wash at a Lake Tahoe Laundromat, I was amazed at the whiteness of the clothes the non-hikers were putting *into* their washers. "Long-distance hikers get used to everything being a dingy gray."

Long-time hiking buddies are like their clothes: well-loved, comfortable, and perfect for the trail.

Hiking as Lifestyle:
Weathercarrot

WEATHERCARROT (1972–) (WC) is one of those people who are so into hiking that he is forever thru-hiking, working trail crew, putting on hiker gatherings, etc. I know him as a master producer of hi-tech slide shows to showcase America's long-distance trails. Even non-hikers are swept away by the excitement he generates.

But the primary reason that the no-fixed-address Weathercarrot deserves recognition is that both his slide shows and his life have always been models of frugality. Because I myself lived for many years on air and water as an unpaid trail worker, I can vouch for the fact that the Carrot is a master of making do. For instance, in 2002 he thru-hiked the entire AT while spending only about $1,100. He later said, "I know that sounds very low and not all that feasible (including all food eaten, postage, new Walkman, pair of new shoes, hostels, and even pizza and ice cream), but for me it has just been a matter of practice over the last twelve years. It's simply a matter of getting yourself used to a certain level of self-discipline. It can even become a game to see how little money you can spend in each town."

I admire WC for extrapolating that frugality to off-the-trail "creative activities that are personally fulfilling and which also benefit other people." His example has been doubly important since the onset of America's worst economic crisis since the Great Depression. When Weathercarrot speaks of the pleasure and sustenance that he finds through "simple living in the midst of a distinct community," I think of all the debt-ridden, foreclosed, jobless people who need a touch of his magic.

Weathercarrot is afloat on the national sea of economic bubbles and bailouts. Come what may, he will continue to paddle unconcerned toward the horizon. I feel comforted to know that he is out there somewhere, enjoying the sky, the sun, and the rain. Each day that he slips by under the radar I want to cheer. Contributing nothing to the GDP but miles hiked, this unassuming thru contributes richly to GDH (gross domestic happiness).

Trail Club Staffer:
Jon Knechtel

JON KNECHTEL (1947–) became a Pacific Northwest Trail Association volunteer in 2001 in order to create color maps of the trail. Then after retiring from Weyerhaeuser in 2003, this former horseman and smoke jumper worked full-time for the group as its director of trail management and subsequently as its acting executive director. Those titles merely hint at the nature of his contribution.

Since I am the PNTA's founder, I might seem to be biased in favor of *any* reasonably competent employee who promotes the development of the trail. Perhaps, but I have chosen Jon as one of my Ten Essentials because he so consistently goes beyond the call of duty to innovate new solutions to our problems. For instance, the club's chief source of funding was until recently its SKY Program, a trail-maintenance employment project for at-risk youth. To keep it and its income stream operating, Jon does everything from recruit team leaders to build bridges to construct signs. Managing SKY is a huge job in itself, but Jon is also always on the move from governmental offices to the halls of Congress.

People often ask him why he puts in seventy- and eighty-hour weeks for so little pay. "I love the Continental Divide to Pacific Ocean concept of the trail," he says, "and I like working with the landowners and the agencies. The part I like least is writing grants, but I do that by necessity. Overall, I have the best job in the world, because I can experience the joy of seeing kids and volunteers on the trail."

The summer of 2008 was an especially tough one; Jon's father died a drawn-out cancer death and his mother broke her back. The PNTA's budgetary shortfalls were worse than usual; its trail crews needed ever more attention. 2009 and 2010 brought a mountain of new work after Congress put its imprimatur on the PNT. Yet Jon was as patient and determined as ever. He said, "Working on the Pacific Northwest Trail makes me happy to get up in the morning. I'm totally committed to developing both the Trail Association and the trail. It's the culmination of my life's work."

Trail Angels:
Ollie Mae Wilson

HOSPITALITY IS an important part of life on the popular "social" trails where the Good Samaritans who assist hikers are called trail angels. Their help usually consists of such things as creating water caches and offering lodging. Some people operate informal shuttle services to provide rides to or from town.

I feel certain that the PCT's most visited trail angels are Donna and Jeff Saufley, whose Hiker Heaven is rightly regarded as a must-stop by every thru-hiker within a hundred miles of Agua Dulce, California. (I have personally witnessed Donna exult at the opportunity to triple-wash stinky visitors' clothes.)

But my own favorite trail angel is Ollie Mae Wilson (1927–), retired postmaster and mayor of Northport, Washington. Her small village (pop. 200) is located where the PNT crosses the Columbia River. In 1983, when my buddy Ted Hitzroth and I walked through, Ollie Mae Wilson put us up. That summer she also hosted another group of six PNT scruffies. Today in her eighties, she explains what happened:

Hikers used to mail supply packages to my post office, and then pick them up when they arrived in town. I remember the first time I actually invited one of them to my home. It was getting late, and, as I was leaving the post office, this very nice fellow showed up to claim his package. I invited him and his hiking partner to shower and have a home-cooked dinner and to pitch their tent in the backyard. They were very impressed that I served some freshly picked wild mushrooms for dinner and that my elderly mother taught them about the area's history.

Becoming a trail angel was an excellent way to meet fascinating types of people that I wouldn't ordinarily have encountered. The thru-hikers always had great stories to tell, and they were Nature people who helped me to see things here in Northport from a different perspective. I never had a bad experience with them, and I would still be a trail angel now if my eyesight weren't failing. All the PNT hikers have been gracious people who fell in love with the natural beauty of this area.

I tell everyone to extend a little hospitality to a hiker because it is good karma that you might need yourself some day!

Battle-hardened Anti-ORV Veterans:
Mark Samsel and Andrew Walters

IN 2000, SOFTWARE DEVELOPMENT MANAGER Mark Samsel (1957–) was settled with his wife Janet and three children in Windham, New Hampshire, a comfortable bedroom community 40 miles north of Boston. His house abutted an abandoned railroad that had been a state-managed multi-use trail since 1985. In the New Hampshire context, "multi-use" meant that all kinds of off-road vehicles were permitted. In the broader southeast New England context, ATVs had already been banned from most Massachusetts jurisdictions, thus funneling them literally toward Mark's doorstep in New Hampshire. Gradually he and two neighbors became more and more alarmed by hundreds of rampaging dirt bikers and ATV riders. "Our pleas for help hit a stone wall with local and state law enforcement. When I was told 'you will never change ORV use on this trail,' the challenge was on." In 2003, Mark, his wife, and neighbors successfully fought back with passage of a bill to restrict mechanized access to the trail. That encouraged them to form the nonprofit Windham Rail Trail Alliance, which raised private funds to pave the trail and to start restoring the old Windham Depot. Today the Windham Rail Trail is unquestionably the benchmark for paved rail-trails in New Hampshire.

In April 2004, Andrew Walters (1961–) and his wife were putting the finishing touches on a three-year restoration of a historic cottage located near a state-owned trail farther west in Fitzwilliam, New Hampshire. One weekend they awoke to a state-sanctioned run of three hundred and fifty ATVs that turned out to be illegal. Since the trail was managed by the New Hampshire Department of Resources and Economic Development (popularly known by the appropriately creepy acronym DRED), Andrew called to complain. "When I questioned them about allowing ATVs on the trail in the future," he said, "they blew me off. Their attitude was: we are in charge here in Concord and what you think really does not matter." However, it did not take long for Andrew to learn that allowing ATVs on the trails was a violation of federal law. He also unearthed the reason for DRED's aggressive push to open public lands to ATVs. In New Hampshire ATV registration fees are used to pay part of the salaries of the same public officials who are in charge of managing the state's recreational trails!

Andrew promptly formed a nonprofit, ATV Watch, to counter the influence which ATV registration fees had bought in the state capital. His theory was that accurate, timely, and complete information was the key to effective action. He pored over laws, regulations, and public officials' statements to ferret out what the secretive DRED was doing. To block him, the department denied him access to public records concerning its ATV trail-development activities. What was initially seen as an issue about ATV use on public lands became an issue about openness in the conduct of public business.

The bottom line is that Mark Samsel and Andrew Walters are the kind of grassroots trails activists that are needed in every county in America.

Singer-songwriter Backpacker:
Walkin' Jim Stoltz

CELEBS RARELY HIKE. The most notorious exception occurred in 2009 when South Carolina's governor, Mark Sanford, purportedly went missing "on the Appalachian Trail." At first I was very excited to think that the tabloids would soon be scouring the AT's summits and hollers for the probable 2012 presidential candidate. The trail was squarely in the news because the ultra-religious Sanford loved hiking so much that he had abandoned his official duties to embark on a secret hike.

It seemed too good to be true—and it was. In reality the horny rascal was never anywhere near the mountains. Instead he was shtupping his mistress in Argentina. For a few weeks the phrase "He's out hiking the Appalachian Trail" became synonymous with illicit sex.

Walkin' Jim Stoltz (1953–2010) was the exact opposite of the *in flagrante delicto* governor. For four footloose decades Jim roamed America with his guitar and his knapsack full of songs. He was *our* celeb. His performances extolled the solitude and magic of wild places. His message was that Nature is something that we carry in our hearts even if we are not in the backcountry.

Sometimes if I am feeling blue, I play my favorite Walkin' Jim tune to remind me of the good life out beyond the trailheads. "With the desert in bloom, and my mind in tune, I've flown my cage, I'm a bird set free," he exulted. Jim was America's troubadour of trails. Just to remember his passionate, heartfelt singing puts a smile on

my face. Jim Stoltz's gravelly voice evoked the thousands of miles of wilderness he explored in a lifetime of rambling. In 2008, he trekked the wild length of the Idaho-Montana border to celebrate the conclusion of his temporarily successful chemotherapy. I think that Walkin' Jim's greatest gift was his ability to share the excitement of the simple act of putting one foot in front of the other.

Jim listened for Nature's music in the deserts and in the mountains, where he tapped into fundamental feelings about the joy of the wilds.

I'm back on the trail again
Missed you like some long lost friend.
Sometimes I think I'm just a part of the
*   wind,*
When I'm back on the trail again.

Walkin' Jim Stoltz was not only our hiker celeb. He was also the voice of the backcountry, the poet of everyone who ever set out from a trailhead. As authentic as muddy boots and well-worn gear, he put our emotions and our hopes into song.

"Very Romantic"

My sex drive had been jammed in neutral for the good part
of the last several weeks. Angela and I had made up after
our Vasquez Rocks blowout but my libido continued to
be beaten down by grime and fatigue. The first night after
Donna's we'd vowed to be more receptive to each other's
physical and emotional needs, but at this point in our trip
regular sex was not one of them.

Duffy Ballard

A Blistered Kind of Love: One Couple's Trial By Trail, 2003

IN EARLY 2006, if I had had any common sense at all, I would
not have asked my girlfriend to join me for a 30-mile winter slog
on the Appalachian Trail. I wanted to interview AT thrus about
their motivations. But being in love, I thought it would be fun
if Christine came along. Since she was not a hiker, I never really
believed that she would accept such a crazy-sounding date. Yet
after I fibbed that it would be "very romantic" she agreed to brave
mountainous northwest Georgia.

In retrospect I don't really know what Tine (*Teen-uh*) saw in
me. My grizzled features contrasted markedly with her dazzling
smile and fluffy brown hair. On the trail, she was a pretty flower
to my scruffy thistle. But it wasn't just her youthful vitality that I
loved. We had so much in common that in the few months we'd
known each other we had already begun to pick up each other's
mannerisms. But I realized too late that the Appalachian Trail had
the potential to drive us apart.

It also risked dangerous falls. Soon after I'd met the vivacious
Dr. Hartmann she'd told me that she was slowly losing her eyesight
from glaucoma. Her vision had already deteriorated so much that
in order to go hiking she had to step carefully and to support herself
with hiking poles.

Though I felt perfectly at home that first night beside a remote, half-frozen brook, Tine recoiled from its desiccated leaves and forlorn trees. Soon she began to get that silent, steamed look that I already knew from past misunderstandings. While she reluctantly donned her new "unattractive" balaclava, I hurried to set up the tent. Then as the temperature plummeted to single digits, I tried to mollify her with a not-found-in-any-restaurant backcountry stew. Luckily for me, she had a raging appetite after climbing 4,461-foot Blood Mountain. After wolfing my slumgullion without complaint, she looked expectantly at me as her breath danced in the headlamp's beam. "What next?" she purred.

I didn't want to be seen as a party pooper, but our skinny mummy bags weren't meant for intimacy. There was also the fact that to save weight I hadn't even brought a jacket or a sweater. I confessed that my after-supper plans were limited to keeping my sleeping bag

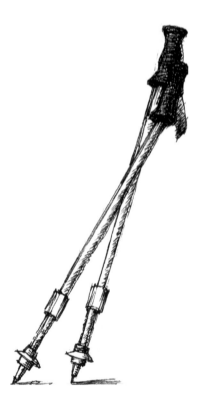

hood cinched so closely around my head that only my nose would show. A very disappointed Tine edged her bag close to mine and switched off her headlamp.

After a while she became aware of an unexpected quality to nights on the trail. The brilliant stars and planets beyond our tent flap were unlike anything she'd ever seen in the city. She was trying to identify constellations when she noticed the aggressive silence that sprang out of the darkness, ready to pounce.

The next thing I knew she was shaking me: "Ron, are you awake?"

"No," I mumbled. "Go to sleep."

"Get up. There's something out there."

My shelter is a 2-pound sil-nylon, hi-tech wonder. Designed for ultralight thru-hiking, it makes little distinction between "out there" and "in here." But, even listening hard, I detected nothing more menacing than the slight rustling of windblown leaves.

"Can't you hear it?" Tine wailed. "It must be a bear."

Oh oh, I thought to myself, worried not about the Big Boy but about the unmistakable panic in my partner's voice. "That's no bear," I assured her sleepily. "It's just ..."

"I'm scared," cried Tine. "I want to go home right now."

"Just close your eyes and pretend you're in a hotel," I said, wishing I had remembered to pack a pair of ear plugs for her.

"No, it's way too scary to stay here. I'm going to start hiking again. If I keep moving, the bears won't bother me. I'll use my headlamp."

The thought of this half-blind neophyte stumbling through the dark-as-a-cave forest finally got my attention. So I suggested, as soothingly as I could, that we scrunch our two bags together in the spoon position. Despite doing that, Tine remained tense. But minutes passed, and I thought that the crisis was over.

Sleeping bags put me to sleep fast. I'd just begun to doze off again when Tine screamed and bolted out into the night. I heard her searching in the dark for her shoes.

By the time I poked my head out she was a hundred feet away. The light from her headlamp registered indecision about which way to run. I knew that if she spooked, I would never be able to find her on that black, moonless mountain.

When she'd originally revealed that she had incurable glaucoma, she'd added, "At night I see even less well." Remembering that now, I feared that disaster was only moments away. She could disappear into the inky wilderness before I even had a chance to squirm out of my bag.

I doubt that anything I said turned her away from the brink. All I know is that she announced that she'd "found a weapon." Then she clambered back inside with her hiking poles. "I will feel better with these beside me," she said patting the two 3-foot-long metal poles. "If a bear tries to get us, I can poke its eyes out."

I hugged her until she slipped away onto the trail of dreams. Thinking of how I had almost lost her, I gently stroked her hair. I realized that I wanted nothing more than to hold her close for the rest of my life.

AT DAWN, BIRD SONG lifted our spirits as we set off along the sunny path. Because I am a long-distance trail developer, I had planned this trip with the express purpose of asking north-bound hikers to explain why each had embarked on a five-month, 2,175-mile quest. Those answers would, I hoped, aid me in designing new trails. Because we walked south into the northbound human wave, stories crested over us with little effort on our part. Our first thru was a bubbly twenty-six-year-old survivor of five surgeries to improve her ankles. Wonderfoot (her trail name) had endured the pain by promising herself to hike the trail until her money gave out. "I want to prove to myself that I can do this hike," she said.

Tine was astonished that any female hiker would attempt to hike the AT alone. I was just into my spiel about hiking's being amazingly safe when along came a fresh-faced twenty-something who looked decidedly non-threatening. "Just plain Joe" peeked out from beneath his humongous maroon backpack and blurted, "How do people get trail names? Do they make them up themselves?"

"No," I said, "usually another hiker, often at the start of your trip, thinks one up for you. But you don't have to accept it. Watch out that somebody doesn't start calling you Red Pack or something equally stupid. The best trail names say something interesting about you."

"What's your trail name?"

"Pathfinder ... because I'm a trail founder. These nicknames are a relatively new thing for backpackers, but they used to be popular on the frontier. They can be a lot of fun."

After the Nameless One had passed, Tine told me that she was certain that he would reach Maine. Despite having no backpacking experience herself, she unhesitatingly gave him a thumbs up because she liked his good-natured attitude. In fact, my lover sized up each of the many dozens of Maine-bound hikers as well as the daytrippers, overnighters, and section hikers who were so numerous that we lost count. When a tiny woman named Willow described the AT as a fortieth-birthday present to herself, Tine, also forty, empathized immediately. Willow (whose pack was at least half as large as she was) said that in low moments she buoyed up her confidence by remembering the many people who had faith in her. "They help me to feel less alone," she said. Small and overloaded, she sometimes felt discouraged by the male twenty-somethings who sped past as if she were standing still. Tine laughed and told Willow that she would meet ten of them "totally wiped" at the nearest pass.

After Willow trudged off toward her destiny, Tine and I stopped at an overlook where wintery north Georgia spread out below. White-painted AT blazes decorated our rock outcrop. Oaks, winter-rimed from the last storm, were reminders of the weather's unpredictability. Dramatic shafts of sunshine shone through the overcast to highlight Appalachian foothills and mountains to the horizon. We grinned like happy fools when our aerie suddenly glowed golden and serene.

Tine was so enchanted by north Georgia's unexpected radiance that when a pair of young newlyweds joined us she became uncharacteristically chatty. Under her questioning, the pair revealed that until recently they'd been counselors at a Rhode Island camp for "at-risk youth." I asked what that meant. "Just that they'd kill you if they had a chance," chuckled the husband, sporting a new trail beard.

After they'd gone, Tine wondered aloud what had attracted them to the trail. The whole enterprise was so beyond her past experience that she was genuinely curious. I winked at her when a second newly hitched couple appeared out of nowhere to answer her question. "We wanted to do something special to celebrate our marriage," said the young man. His wife's face lit up like our Georgia sunbeams. "We've been married for three days and we love the AT." As soon as they were out of sight, Tine gave them, too, a hearty thumbs up. I agreed. But it wasn't just their infectious love that impressed me. They were also much better prepared than most newbies, with lightweight, carefully chosen gear.

Sensible planning can easily make the difference between an aborted trek and a successful thru-hike. And we were about to meet the poster boy of foolish packing. I'll just call him Sad Sack. Even from a distance I could tell by his limp that he was in trouble. Up close I noticed that his huge burden listed badly to starboard. Loose shoulder straps and tighteners aggravated his poor balance. Worst of all, Sad Sack's waist belt (which should have supported his load on his hips) dangled around his thighs like a pendulous skirt. He mumbled that he planned to adjust everything that evening when he had "more time."

If you make it that far! I thought.

Sad Sack explained that he had a "long, thin torso" and that his waist belt was cinched as tightly as possible. "This is the best I could do," he said. "I *needed* this size pack."

After he left, Tine was astonished that any store would have sold him something so ill fitting. "How can he begin a 2,400-mile journey with so little forethought?" she proclaimed, as much to the rocks and trees as to me.

AS WE DOVE INTO the trail's stream of northbound pilgrims, we met people who'd dreamed of exploring the AT for as long as they could remember. For the two superannuated buddies who basked in each other's company, friendship was the deciding factor. For the pair of impressionable nineteen-year-old J. R. R. Tolkien fans, adventure was the thing. Some folks cited "personal growth," while others eagerly anticipated a beer-fueled, endless party.

The more narratives we heard, the more we noticed that they often centered upon people's search for a better future. But, I wondered, what about the non-hikers back home? How did they differ from these trekkers? My guess was that what prevented the stay-at-homes from hiking had far more to do with attitudinal rather than practical impediments. It was probably less that they didn't have the time and/or the means than that they feared that hiking might be dirty, difficult, or even dangerous.

Tine herself had felt that way before I used unfair advantage to lure her into the woods. So I was surprised the morning after the Georgia trip when she said that she'd had such a good time that she would like to go backpacking again. "Just to have nothing to do but walk and eat and sleep felt so good," she said. "To do that with the one person on earth I love most was like a miracle for me in my stressful life."

Off the Trail: Walden Pond

I now face a life that is, like everyone's life, filled with trail intersections, with unmarked spots where I don't know which way the trail goes, and with the awful uncertainty that accompanies a world where choice is infinite. And with all the beauty that infinite choice offers, I miss—more than I could have imagined—a world where my only choices involved where to stop for the night and which flavor of Lipton dinner to eat for each meal.

Scott Huler, "Bringing the Trail's Lessons Back To Life,"
in *The News & Observer*, Raleigh, North Carolina
May 22, 1995

I MET TINE, then thirty-nine, the old-fashioned way, via the Internet. I was looking for a backpacking partner with whom to explore the Sea-To-Sea Route. Instead I found a four-star hotel maven whose interest in trails was minimal but whose tolerance for me was both unexpected and very welcome. She and I had both been hitched before and had a sense of the compromises inherent in marriage. So forsaking thirty years of nomadism, I decided to propose to her on Valentine's Day at Walden Pond, home of my hero Henry David Thoreau.

Since a proposal is one of the few acts in life for which there is little or no guidance, I mass-e-mailed my friends for advice. The resulting hilarity showed that many people doubted that marriage was part of my vocabulary. Their suggestions ranged from the quaint (hide the ring in a snowman) to the literary (read aloud to her from Thoreau's *Journals*). My recently divorced buddy Keith Clark wrote from Anchorage to warn, "*I* got married on Valentine's Day. *Don't do that.* Hard to get dinner reservations every year, and now, it really sucks as a remembrance."

"Bah humbug, to you, Keith," I thought. However, on V-Day, fate intervened with the winter's most hellacious snowstorm. Blowing every which way, the blizzard convinced Tine that travel was too dangerous. That coincided with my learning that Walden Pond was not the bucolic retreat popularized by my hero Henry D. Actually it was a state park with 9-5 hours and zillions of recreationists who were prohibited from parking anywhere but in the $5 lot that closed at 5 p.m. So Valentine's Day was out. However, the next evening Mr. Romantic decided to lead an outlaw expedition in the dark to declare his love.

The object of my affections was decidedly uninterested in trudging to Walden by headlamp. Thoreau held no more appeal for her than the smell of unbathed thrus. Nevertheless, the night after Valentine's we found ourselves on busy Walden Street south of Concord. The only light came from the glare of oncoming headlights. To avoid being hit we slogged along a high berm into the frostbite wind while the snow squeaked loudly under our boots. Halfway to the park, Tine balked. What was the point of risking our lives on that dangerous road? Why couldn't we be in a warm restaurant ordering something tasty? That somehow reminded me that both Thoreau and his brother John had proposed unsuccessfully to the same girl. If Walden's greatest hero had been shot down, what chance did sorry Strickland have?

Tine felt hungry and cold and frightened by the incessant traffic. But I explained that the evening's associations with Thoreau were important to me, so she gamely gave it another try. We continued south across the Concord Turnpike's river of cars. Soon we were in deep woods and crunching along a snowy trail in search of the pond. Dressed in Golite down parkas and rain pants, we defied the temperature and the wind. I was excited by my mission and by the sense that I was where the American conservation movement had begun.

Tine's mood brightened as soon as she saw the lake's flat white expanse bordered by its ring of dark hills. As a Mount Holyoke undergraduate, she had loved winter ponds so much that she'd spent many hours peering at their ice-entombed leaves and bubbles.

So when she found Walden's expanse of snow-covered ice, she forgot her earlier reservations about my daft date. She ran out into the middle of the pond and flopped down on her back to drink in the stars.

I lay beside her, aware of the vast silence between us and Venus on the western horizon. Walden seemed almost a part of the familiar constellations overhead. Snow cushioned my hips and head. Feeling at home, as I always do in the wilds, I sought the courage to tell Tine what she had meant to me. "Our whole is greater than the sum of our parts," I stumbled, aware that any words sounded insignificant in such a magnificent setting. *Keep it short*, I thought. So I reached for her gloved hand, and simply said that I loved her and wanted to marry her.

She hesitated so long that I became aware of the cold seeping up from the snow and ice. My fingers began to throb painfully; my heart pounded. What would Tine say? I suddenly realized that I truly had no idea what her response would be.

The moments stretched by interminably. I began to fear that maybe I was making a fool of myself.

Finally she blurted, "Yes, I will marry you."

The relief I felt boomed through my mind like a giant crack in the ice. We embraced despite the barriers of our puffy coats. When we kissed, I felt lost in a dream. *Yes, I will marry you,* she'd said. I wondered if I could both make her happy and wean myself from my nomadic lifestyle.

"Yes," she said again. And, as if reading my thoughts, she added, "It will be the beginning of many exciting new trails."

"For I Believed in Traveling Light"

The north exerts a profound attraction on the armchair imaginations of many Japanese people, because it epitomizes what they call furusato, "the old home country," and its influence on their lives. The Tōhoku [Region] of their imagination is a perfect furusato, a place that is content to be old-fashioned, that doesn't alter with each new twist of "progress," where nature, though harsh, is also generous, and where time is measured by the changes of the seasons.

Alan Booth
The Roads To Sata: A 2,000-Mile Walk Through Japan, 1985

"IS HE A FAMOUS ACTOR?" The agent at the Japan Airlines counter at JFK had been extremely solicitous. Then as soon as I'd stepped away to find the rest room, he'd blurted out his question to Tine. "No, that's my husband," Tine answered, dumbfounded. "If he were a celebrity, why would we be flying Economy Class for thirteen hours to Tokyo?"

"That's what they all say," he said. "Famous actors often fly in the rear of the plane so that they won't be recognized. Are you sure he isn't an actor? He looks a lot like Klin-toh."

"Who?" asked Tine.

"Klin-toh Eastoh-woodoh." He smiled conspiratorially. "I am a big fan of Dirty Harry."

Okay, if you must know, my super-tidy wife often calls me Dirty (as in grungy) Ron. But Dirty Harry? The frequency with which people mistook me for Klin-toh was only one of many cross-cultural surprises in store for me in October 2008 during our belated honeymoon in the land of the Rising Sun.

Tine wanted to reconnect with old friends. I hoped to use hiking as a passport to understand Japan. And although my language proficiency was limited to *"toilet wah, doh-koh des kah?"* (Where

181

is the toilet?), I had an ace in the hole in Tine who was so fluent (after living in Japan's Toh-hoku region for ten years) that whenever she spoke Japanese on the phone, people assumed from her accent that she was a native speaker.

EVEN BEFORE the bullet train dropped us off in Iwate, I fell in love with the appearance of the northern prefecture where Tine had spent her twenties. If it hadn't been for the rice paddies and tin-roofed homes, I would have sworn that I was speeding across western Puget Sound's Skagit Flats. Scattered, undeveloped hills and mountains punctuated the flat, fertile farmlands. A multitude of rivers reminded me of the Snohomish, Stillaguamish, Skagit, and Samish. In other words, unlike in Tokyo, where I felt very much the outsider, in Iwate I sensed an immediate kinship with the landscape.

I'd long heard the story of Tine's 1987 arrival in the town of Misusawa as its first resident Western woman. Wherever she went swarms of kids used to tag after her shouting, "*Gaijin da!*" [There's a foreigner!] That never happened to me because by 2008 even rural Japan was much more used to seeing non-Japanese on the streets.

I was favorably impressed that everyone remembered *Hah-toh-mahn-san* (Hartmann) as a warm, beloved teacher and good friend. At the wedding reception that her old colleagues and mentors held for us in a Misusawa restaurant, person after person (some teary-eyed) rose to tell anecdotes about her contributions to the town and to their lives.

Neither Tine nor I had realized before traveling to Misusawa and walking its rice-paddy-bordered lanes just how much she used to try to "become Japanese." Having spent summer vacations in Germany as a child and been accepted as a German, she had wanted to achieve the same degree of acceptance in Japan as a twenty-something. But that was then and this was 2008. Her doctorate, two marriages, academic research, and the loss of her parents all were a lifetime removed from the twenty-two-year-old gushily enthusiastic *Hah-toh-mahn-san* that the Iwate folk remembered. On this return visit she saw only a distant image of her old self as reflected in the eyes of people whose lives had changed relatively little.

Just before Tine and I left Iwate, we walked across Misusawa to visit her favorite restaurant, Gorozushi. It was obvious even to me that the area had fallen on hard times. Tine was shocked by the downtown's lack of pedestrians, bicycles, and small automobiles. "People don't like these old-fashioned shops," she said, "that lack parking and where there's always a long palaver instead of a quick transaction." I was about to witness exactly what she meant.

After we pushed our way past the hole-in-the-wall's entrance curtain, we surprised the seventy-year-old proprietor and his assistants in the middle of their afternoon break. Everyone was watching a melodrama on a huge, high-def TV. As soon as they recognized Tine, all three bowed and burst into expansive smiles. "*Hah-toh-man-san*, how are you?" they called. The owner was an erect, impish little man who insisted that we sit at the counter, drink green tea, and watch while he prepared some of his best sushi. After I said that I had been looking forward to meeting him, he beamed and repaid my compliment with an exquisite piece of raw fish.

Though my wife had not lived in Misusawa for twelve years, she joined the fun as if she had only stepped away the previous week. Tine had been such a Gorozushi habitue that no one seemed surprised when she asked about such and such a relative or favorite customer. My participation in the conversation was limited by my need for translation and by my hunger for one delicacy after another. But even without understanding what was said I loved the mood of joshing, free-form hilarity.

The master was a fifty-year veteran of sushi making. In a cosmopolitan American city, his small restaurant would have been a gold mine. Here we enjoyed a command performance as his hands effortlessly formed little rolls of, for instance, rice and salmon eggs. When Tine gave him a German-made figurine of a chef, his old eyes lit up in genuine gratitude.

That fabulous lunch, one of the best of my life, was on him, he said at its close. "A wedding present from me to *Hah-toh-man-san* and her husband."

Afterward I towered over everyone else as we posed for photos outside his cloth-draped entrance. The now-unfashionable street was deserted save for a trio of old ladies. I was very touched by the master's affection for my wife, but when Tine waved a final time from the end of his block, she turned the corner on her old life. From now on her life in the United States would be paramount.

THE JAPANESE ALPS were introduced to the West by an English missionary mountaineer named Walter Weston (1861–1940) who in 1891 hiked a drovers' track over an obscure pass to a remote section of the Azusa River. In 1896, he described the spectacular Kamikohchi Valley and its surrounding peaks in *Mountaineering and Exploring in the Japanese Alps*. Weston later helped protect the region from logging and grazing. I was fascinated during our five-day stay in the region to discover parallels with America's own John Muir.

Unlike Weston, who entered Kamikohchi by shank's mare, Tine and I rode a large bus through a series of tunnels to our hotel. There we looked out upon a pond that dated from 1915, when mudflows from a stratovolcano named Yake-dake (8,054 feet) had dammed the Azusa River. Though Yake-dake (or Burning Peak) looked peaceful, it had killed people as recently as 1995.

Hiking in the Kamikohchi Valley rivaled Tokyo for congestion, but we were so eager to see the magnificent environment that we plunged into the human stream of camera-toting oldsters. Like a band of Chaucerian pilgrims we marched several miles *en masse* past hotels, hostels, campsites, and gift shops to the post office and visitors center. (I learned later that the river trail's traffic counter averaged five thousand per day.)

Next morning Tine and I were determined to escape the crowds. I was in my element as the North Cascades-like mountains beckoned. Hiking fast, we rapidly outdistanced dozens of slow-moving Japanese seniors. Tine cleared our path, repeating "Excuse me" in Japanese. After trying to identify the larches, pines, and maples, I hurried to catch up. I raced between a trail-wide puddle and the bamboo undergrowth, only to trip on a hidden stump. My momentum carried me forward in a beautiful arc: head first into the mud.

Stunned, I lay face down in wet gravel, and gingerly moved my legs and arms. "*Daijohbu?*" people cried as they gathered around my prostrate form. "Are you all right?"

Tine urged me to return to the hotel but I, not wanting to cancel our long-anticipated hike, insisted on going to the nearby river to wash myself off. She followed me to the shallows, but thought that I was so scratched and bloody that we needed help. So she approached a half-dozen elderly picnickers who were making coffee over a camp stove. "My husband fell and hurt himself," she said in Japanese. "Do you have any antiseptic, please?"

Everyone looked to their camera-festooned teacher for a response. He said that Tine should bring me to them for bandaging. They were, he explained, a group of amateur poets to whom he was teaching the verse form known as *tanka*. I smiled inwardly to think that of all the park's vast crowds of people I was about to be rescued by poets.

After a retired nurse patched me up, things were looking good until I stumbled yet again. This time I fell metaphorically on my face with a resounding diplomatic thud.

My grand gaffe began innocently enough when I thanked each person with a formal presentation of my business card. Having read about that procedure before our trip, I felt confident I could use it to make a good impression. First I gave one to the nurse, being careful to hold it with two hands so that the writing faced her in the approved manner. She beamed gratefully, bowed, and gave it attention worthy of the Rosetta Stone.

When I tried the same drill with the husband of one of the women, I noticed the teacher pop off a snapshot of us. Unfortunately, that activated my uncontrollable penchant for posed portraits. Without thinking, I yelled, "No, no," at him and grabbed my business card back from the startled husband.

I was about to suggest that we restage the whole interaction when Tine grabbed my hand to intervene. "*What* are you doing?" she cried, too late, snatching the card and pressing it back into the man's hands. But the damage had been done.

"*Hah-toh-mahn-san*, why did he take it back?" moaned the crestfallen husband in Japanese. The poor fellow looked mortally hurt. Ideally, the ritualistic exchange of business cards combines samurai sensitivity with balletic grace. But I, horrible foreigner, had managed to insult everyone. Even Tine's linguistic and diplomatic talents could not paper over such louche behavior.

Luckily I redeemed myself with Tine by taking her on some fun climbs up a series of fixed ladders to Yake-dake's sulphur-smelling crags. Though she enjoyed the otherworldly swirling mists of volcanic steam, she did look a little green.

With the very different fog of cross-cultural misunderstanding fresh on my mind, I asked some Canadian, Italian, Czech, and Dutch hikers on the Yake-dake Trail if they could communicate adequately in Japan without knowing Japanese. All agreed that the locals' were only able to communicate on simple subjects in English. It made me appreciate anew just how lucky I was to have Tine as my interpreter. Though Japanese children invariably study English, they rarely emerge into adulthood fluent in the language of Shakespeare and Randy Newman. The problem is exacerbated by their having been taught "Japanese English" to conform to their familiar consonant and vowel sounds. Thus, my supposed look-alike's name was always pronounced Klin-toh Eastoh-woodoh.

That is not to say that Tine and I did not meet Japanese hikers whose English was excellent. For instance, I spoke with a retired electronics manufacturing executive who'd spent three years in Texas. Upon hearing that I wanted to sleep overnight in a mountain hut, he suggested the one at Tokugoh Pass (2,135 meters), the "oldest and most historic" in the Japanese Alps. So off we went. After climbing a beautifully graded, nicely switchbacked trail, Tine and I arrived at the Tokugoh Hut at 3:30 on a Thursday afternoon. Despite the haze, I could see deep enough into the park's rugged interior to begin to dream of a future hike that would tie together as many of its high trails as possible.

We were greeted by the hut's master and his "sub support" assistant. They explained that the old wooden structure had originally been built as a hunting camp "in the year twelve of the Taishoh emperor," i.e., in 1923. That it was standing at all seemed like a miracle. Massive beams propped up the walls to prevent their collapse under the weight of the snow that buried the hut each winter.

We left our boots at the entrance and padded about in stockinged feet on tatami mats. The master graciously let Tine and me sleep on the downstairs floor so that I would be less likely to crack my head on the low beams of the loft. He also favored everyone that

evening with a special homemade stew. There were only five other dinner guests, though weekends apparently saw upward of twenty-five or so. Four out of five of our fellow hikers were middle-aged or elderly women. One seventy-year-old grandmother told us that she still hiked all over the Japanese Alps alone. Everyone agreed that it was common for women to hike solo or in small groups.

At supper, we seven sat cross-legged at the long, low table on which our dinner bubbled in two crockery pots. Some of the women had brought vegetables that they stirred into the mountain stew with their chopsticks. Our seventy-year-old wonder woman had even hauled up two eggs as her contribution. Tine and I had nothing to donate except money (lodging was expensive) and Tine's unique perspective as a Japanese-speaking *gaijin*.

Two gas lanterns bathed the hut with their warm glow. I loved everything, from the delicious spring water to the typical hiker talk about favorite trails, foods, and huts. Our five new friends confessed (in Japanese) that whenever they saw a *gaijin* on the trails they fled for fear of having to resurrect their long-forgotten high school English. ("Thank you, Tine," I thought to myself yet again.)

I was fascinated to learn that the master had originally been a *salaryman*. Thirty years earlier, as a respite from his cubicle existence, he had begun assisting the then-master with chores. Eventually he had succumbed to the hut's mystique and had taken the job himself. When, after supper, we guests retired to our futons and I heard him closing the hut down for the night, I wondered if a young person would come along to carry on the tradition.

At midnight I rose quietly and snuck outside to drink in the moonlight that flooded my uncrowded corner of twenty-first-century Japan. Walter Weston must have seen the same sight in 1891. In fact, he wrote: "The view from near the highest point of the pass is one of the grandest in Japan, so intensely does it differ in character from the ordinary mountain landscapes with their rounded outlines and verdure-clad slopes."

Culture is what you make of it, I thought. The past and the future were not necessarily more romantic or desirable than our own time. Out in the night air, I understood why some people earlier in the day had not wanted us foreigners to visit the hut for fear of the bad impression that its rustic appearance might make. However, I loved the fact that it was so authentic that until recently its meals had been cooked over an indoor fire pit. But what I liked best about the Tokugoh Pass Hut was not its construction or its 2,135-meter elevation. The antique structure sheltered a precious conviviality that more advanced parts of Japan had sometimes lost. Our visit reminded me that the simple act of walking is often a passport to the country of the heart.

AFTER RETURNING from my midnight ramble I was unable to sleep because I kept thinking about a friend who—in love with Norway—had long wanted to ski the length of that country. The previous February he'd gone missing over there. Eventually a hunter had found John McLaughlin's decomposed body on an exposed ridge deep in a national park. My buddy had died several miles off course during a forty-year blizzard while attempting to fulfill his lifelong dream of skiing from the Baltic to the Arctic. Two decades earlier I'd jokingly dubbed him *Rasta* Johan because he was totally bald. I called him "Johan" simply because that was the Norwegian version of John. Five years after we met in 1982, he thru-hiked the Pacific Northwest Trail. He was a stubborn, generous, and devoted friend. I missed his funny laugh and even his habit of peppering his letters with Norwegianisms. People told me that he died doing something that he loved. But I couldn't help but dwell upon his probable terror when he realized that he was irretrievably lost and so cold that he couldn't even set up his tent.

The morning after my midnight excursion at Tokugoh Pass I met someone whose own bereavement distracted me from mine. Tine and I had decided to walk a few miles upstream along the Azusa River in order to draw out our last hours in less crowded parts of Kamikohchi. As usual I was lagging behind, this time photographing a troop of wild monkeys. I never captured anything but monkey butt, but was almost distracted from noticing a middle-aged woman who plodded up to me under an enormous backpack. I was about to inundate her with advice about lightweight gear when I remembered that I didn't even know the Japanese word for heavy. I opened my mouth only to make an idiotic grin. There was nothing for me to do but point at her pack and do my best Sisyphus imitation. That predictably got nowhere. By the time I caught up with Tine at a megahut, I had forgotten about the overburdened hiker.

At the *Hütte* (hiking vocabulary tends to be Swiss-based in Japan), I learned that such establishments can lodge as many as six hundred and fifty people in a mix of everything from dorms to private rooms. Hikers are cosseted with Muzak, gift shops, and green tea ice cream. Of course, I felt pretty smug about having stayed at the Tokugoh Pass Hut instead. But in retrospect I understand the need for such mass tourism facilities for a population of 127 million that is crammed into a land area smaller than California's.

Back outside, we unexpectedly encountered the hiker whom I'd met earlier. Setting up her tent on the lawn, Tazuko, sixty, was so eager to talk with Tine that I never did get to pester her about the latest gear. She explained that she used to backpack all over Japan with her late husband. But after his death two and a half years earlier, she'd been so depressed that she hadn't hiked again until now. Tine, learning more details, was quite touched by our new friend's loss. We were both delighted when she invited us to her home, which happened to be in the suburbs of our next destination, Kyoto.

After several days of sightseeing, we fetched up at Tazuko's house. She told us that she had married very young and then lived with her husband's tradition-bound mother. That nineteenth-century-born dowager had influenced Tazuko not only to wear a kimono daily but also to adopt other old-fashioned ways. As a result our new friend had devoted her life to Mamoru, her late husband.

Japanese homes often contain an altar to commemorate the family's ancestors. There's usually a statue of the Buddha as well as food offerings and some of the deceased's small personal items. But in a sense, Tazuko's entire house was such a memorial, since her professor husband's slippers, toothbrush, comb, and papers were still its emotional center. But what struck me most forcefully was that her official altar contained not just his photos and knickknacks but also the half-empty pack of Marlboros he'd been smoking on the day that he died of lung cancer.

When I had impulsively spoken to Tazuko on that trail in Kamikohchi, she was struggling with a far greater burden in her heart than that on her back. Meeting me had coincided with her brave, halting attempt to emerge from two and a half years of extreme grief. Her experience reminded me that I still hadn't come to grips with the loss of my friend Rasta Johan. What would be an appropriate memorial? Certainly I had always been profoundly thankful to him, one of our earliest Pacific Northwest Trail thru-hikers, for having stuck with me when very few people believed in my dream. After returning from Japan, I spoke to John's father and brother Tim with a proposal to erect a John McLaughlin hiker shelter somewhere along the Pacific Northwest Trail.

And, speaking of the unexpected, Tine and I hadn't been home in Massachusetts long when someone in Japan sent us a mysterious 13-foot-long parchment scroll. It turned out that one of the Tanka poets was a calligrapher. Remembering my interest in long-distance walking, seventy-year-old Kumiko had copied out a portion of *Narrow Road to the Deep North*, an account of a 1689 trip, much of it on foot, made by Matsuo Basho (1644–1694), Japan's greatest haiku master. My favorite passage described his walk to Yoshino in search of cherry blossoms. Like a modern thru-hiker, he

threw away quite a number of things, for I believed in traveling light. There were certain things, however, I had to carry on my back—such as a raincoat, an overcoat, an inkstone, a brush, writing paper, medicine, a lunch basket—

and these constituted quite a load for me. I made such
slow progress that I felt deeply depressed as I walked along
with faltering steps, giving as much power as I could to my
trembling knees.

Tired of walking
I put up at an inn,
Embraced comfortably
By wisteria flowers.

The scroll was bewitchingly beautiful. But there was another treat in its box. I found a note written in careful English penmanship that said, "We were glad to meet you through your big happening here. My hobby is tanka and calligraphy. I have been doing them for about forty years. I want to show you one of my tanka called Kamikohchi."

Asa yū ni kiri no misogi o ukenagara
Kamikohchi no aki zo fukamaru

Tine translated that as:

Soaked each morning and evening
in purifying fog,
Kamikohchi's autumn
deepens.

INTERNATIONAL TRAVEL can teach us a lot about ourselves. I went to Japan to learn what I could about hiking there. But I soon began to wish that I were as good a man as Basho, who "believed in traveling light" and who followed up on it better than I ever did. I used to think it hilarious that people mistook me for Klin-Toh Eastoh-Woodoh since I looked nothing like that actor and since I totally lacked his angry screen persona. But thinking back to his fans' misplaced enthusiasm reminds me now of the fun that Tine and I had with it. People who know Tine call her a "beacon of cheerfulness." And our Japan adventure confirmed me in my role as her most ardent fan.

Nowadays I am mostly "off the trail," as that ultimate thru-hiker Basho might have said. And, like him, I feel the attraction of adventure and Nature as much as ever. It's just that my heart is large enough now to have room for both hiking and for growing old with my bride, *Hah-toh-mahn-san.*

The Path Ahead

*Four million users of the Appalachian Trail from all over
the country are clearly crying out for more trails and less
use on each one. The question then is, "Do we want four
millions users on our special trail?" And, of course, the
answer is that if there are more trails, the impact on any one
is reduced. That is what the Pacific Crest and the AT need;
they need other trails so that no one bears all the load.*

Paul Pritchard, Executive Director
Appalachian Trail Conference,
letter to the author, September 1, 1976

WITHOUT ENOUGH NEWBIES to walk our trails, they will
disappear back into the brush. Without a future where trails are
cherished, Nature itself will increasingly be at risk. Where then will
we find the next generation of trail users?

I am discouraged by reports that people are less and less
interested in non-electronic activities such as hiking. But at the
same time my bibliography is bursting with trail authors whose
exuberance is evident in their titles. *Follow the White Blazes.
White Blaze Fever. Alone in the Appalachians. A Journey North.
Walking North. Walking Home. Walking the Dream. You Won't
Get to Maine unless You Walk in the Rain.* These cheerful souls are
going places, and they are traveling there on foot.

The publishing industry may be headed south, but self-publishing
and the Internet have enabled hiker creativity to flourish. Print on
demand ensures that anyone can fit her tale between two covers,
and blogging is another popular choice. Even lowly e-mails can
take wing as books (as is proved by *Bearfoot, A Northbounder:
E-mails from the Appalachian Trail.*) Hiking literature—at its
best—reminds me of campfire storytelling's magical realm of
adventure. This is the spirit that will sustain vast numbers of future
trail fans.

ONE CHILLY NORTH CASCADES morning in 1970, I was dreaming peacefully in my sleeping bag, soothed by the music of Cutthroat Creek, when the rumble of heavy machinery awoke me. Half asleep, I heard someone shout, "Move your tent, Mister. I need to bulldoze where you are."

Peering outside, I saw a burly, unsmiling man in a hard hat. "You've got to be kidding," I protested. But the intruder was dead serious about rearranging my bedroom with his big yellow Cat. And that was how I became an unwilling participant in the construction of the North Cross State Highway, a two-lane mountain road between north-central Washington and saltwater. From the environmentalist point of view, that highway was a massive boondoggle. It cost a fortune then, and snow closes it every winter now. But I am still impressed by its promoters' success. They understood what they wanted, and they went after it.

You have to know your destination to be able to get there. My immodest goal for the National Trails System is to better serve twenty-first-century hikers. To do so I propose to:

1. *Develop the transcontinental Sea-To-Sea Route.* Canada has the Trans Canada Trail, and the United States should have a Sea-To-Sea Route. The vision is large, and the benefits are many, beginning with the chance to transform our helter-skelter National Trails System into something that more clearly approximates a true network.

As a practical matter, the 7,700-mile Sea-To-Sea Route is already almost complete. We just need three additional links in Vermont, Montana, and North Dakota. Development of C2C is eminently doable. Looking beyond the practical to the symbolic, I think of C2C as a modern-day Northwest Passage, complete with ocean surf, grand prairies, and mountain passes. Everyone from dayhikers to thrus will step a little more jauntily just to know that he or she is part of such a magnificent trail.

2. *Expand the number of North America's major long-distance trails.* Creating new national scenic trails requires two acts of Congress. I see no reason why the process must be so arduous and so skewed toward disqualifying new trails. There must be a better way to vet potential entrants such as the Highlands Trail (New York–New Jersey), the California Coastal Trail, or the Mountains-to-Sea Trail (North Carolina).

As mentioned earlier, national scenic trail status offers the best long-term protection for long-distance trails. To qualify, a trail should ideally be multi-state, very long, and highly scenic. Such routes tend to traverse spectacular backcountry and be limited to hikers (and sometimes equestrians). However, there are plenty of trails that might not be suitable as *national scenic trails* but that need protection and that might make superb additions to the National Trails System if there were a new category called *greenway trail.* An example would be the East Coast Greenway (ECG), an in-progress, 3,000-mile, multi-use, non-motorized route that will eventually connect Calais, Maine, with Key West, Florida. Today the ECG benefits thousands of people who follow its attractive conifer-design signs across towns, suburbs, and country. The success of the East Coast Greenway Alliance in places like  Portland, Maine, Boston, Massachusetts, and New York shows that *greenway trails* could radically expand the populations served by the National Trails System.

I propose that we create many new multimodal walking, hiking, jogging, biking, and cross-county skiing trails *where people actually live.* Towns such as Corvallis, Oregon, have proved that the public will readily use this type of resource if public officials are wise enough to build it. I love the example of rail-trails. As soon as a new one opens, parents push strollers, dog owners walk pets, commuters commute, and in-line skaters swish and swoop.

For many years I was mainly interested in backcountry, mountainous trails. However, I am now also a fervent supporter of suburban trails. A good example is the Charles River Link, a new (2009) 16-mile route west of Boston. I agree with Link founder Denny Nackoney, who told me recently that suburban trails are "the future of hiking in the United States. If people get out to enjoy the open spaces, then they will have a feeling of ownership and want to protect that experience for the future."

3. Create a National Trails Center. The National Trails System is neither an independent organization nor a physical address. There is nowhere that I can go to visit its nonexistent director or headquarters. Yet this shadow entity is responsible for an ever-growing list of national scenic, national recreation, and national historic trails. It is as if the Defense Department had no Pentagon.

The solution is to create a National Trails Center in Washington, DC, to enhance the role of trails in American life. I envision it as an independent congressionally funded NGO, modeled perhaps on the America's Byways Resource Center in Duluth, Minnesota. Such a center could research, plan, promote, assist, manage, and, to some extent, fund the components of the National Trails System. The result would be better public access, greater standardization (in such things as signage), and, most importantly, increased public awareness of trails and hiking.

And while we're at it, let's follow the model of the Appalachian Trail and make sure that *all* "national scenic trails" are "units" of the National Park System. Bringing them under one umbrella agency could theoretically lead to better management and greater equity in the distribution of federal resources.

TRAILS OFFER US as much fun as we have wit to enjoy. Few things cost so little but give pleasure to so many. Trails are a resource for the future and a link to the past. The word *trail* suggests fitness and adventure. There is no hint in that word of gloom or failure.

I am optimistic about trails, and I am excited each time that I meet someone for whom the hiking world is fresh with possibility. In fact, I believe that the National Trail System's second fifty years could be a Golden Age of North American hiking. I want to be there to help make it happen.

Along the PNT: Shared Vision

The trail itself even seems to have a therapeutic value, as if, by touching it, by walking along it, we absorb the magic of its freedom, the freshness of its air, the inspiration of the forest rebirth. Like Antaeus, we are renewed.

Ann and Myron Sutton
The Appalachian Trail: Wilderness on the Doorstep, 1967

TINE'S GLAUCOMA is gradually destroying her sight. My "beacon of cheerfulness" has faced this with humor and courage, but I am worried for her. Since she is more than twenty years younger than I am, she may be totally blind after I am already permanently "off the trail." This causes me great heartache. Who will care for her when I am gone? She assures me that she will be okay and that she will always be able to see, "if not with the eyes, then with my heart."

In this chapter (a trailside love letter), I propose an imaginary "Last Hike" for the two of us to the Continental Divide.

DEAR TINE, we are no longer in shape to hike the northern Rockies. But instead of vigor, we still have imagination. So please picture yourself with me in Glacier National Park at the summer solstice. You and I will climb 2,000 feet in 2.3 miles to Brown Pass at 6,255 feet.

Don't worry. I have some of that German rye bread and Gruyere cheese that you like. You won't go hungry. There are few bugs and no people: only bears who've awakened from their winter naps. And I have brought along your trusty hiking poles.

On our gradual way up, west, we feel reborn to hear creeks laugh their greetings. June sun penetrates the morning chill. High above us, miles-thick sedimentary layers are alive with torrents of water that flash and jump down the snowy buttresses and between the horizontal bands of dark fir and brilliant white. Braided creeks crash from the heights in wind-tossed strands of foam. Our spirits exult in the water's infectious music.

The season's vital new life is adrift in the diaphanous currents of pollen, streaming from fir and spruce. Underfoot, the spiky blue flowers of bee balm contrast with the familiar five petals of phlox and the broad leaves of false hellebore. Menziesia thickets extend long arms into the trail where their clusters of thin, pale green leaves can get full sun.

In a sense, you and I seek the sun, too, as we climb toward the pass. However, our westering route gains elevation slowly. Patches of sunshine envelop us in the warm scent of fir needles. Vernal flowers bedeck our way. Mats of red alder sport new sprouts and catkins. A raven flaps up-valley, skirting subalpine firs. A white, delicately marked butterfly flutters among elk droppings. Clumps of mountain ash berries brighten our path with splashes of orange color.

In Glacier National Park, each species has a strategy to withstand the crushing weight of snow. Alders and mountain ashes bend submissively; subalpine firs arrow into the sky.

Where a channel erodes the trail into a wide, rocky sluiceway, springy alders clutch at our packs and threaten to force us into the torrent. "Holy cow!" you cry as you jump the flood and continue excitedly uphill on dry trail.

We feel the cold downdrafts that cascade onto us from dark clouds ahead. I want to linger in the sun, but you—always the good planner—urge me to speed up to reach the pass before the coming storm. So we leave tracks across patches of snow where the yellow beauty of glacier lilies hints at the coming of spring.

A trout darts upstream as fog begins to hide the buttes. Freeze-damaged catkins hang black and lifeless. At a snowed-in gully, I witness a pliable branch spring free from the ice.

We pass another lake just in time to see a mallard drake burst noisily into the air. Shorebirds decorate a half-submerged log. A scruffy deer emerges warily from the brush to nibble. I want to discuss it all, but I reluctantly agree not to dawdle.

I am glad when, breathing hard, we stop to take in the full magnificence of the upper valley, half in sun, half in the storm's dark grip. Gawking at the remains of a four-hundred-foot slab avalanche, I say that I love hiking with you. Your kiss is the perfect response.

Our sunny mood endures despite the interruption of large raindrops that splat on our bare arms. We keep walking until forced to stop to pull out our umbrellas and rain gear. It takes only an instant for small hailstones to whiten the trail. They delight you with their ricocheting "jolly spectacle." That happy insouciance intensifies my pleasure. The only thing better than loving what I do is doing it with the person I love.

After the squall slips away as quickly as it came, buttes and spires emerge from the inky clouds. Sweat trickles down our faces as we climb cautiously cross-country toward the dark pass. Stunted, wind-rattled firs produce an eery sound from every direction at once. Stalks of last year's bear grass rattle in the stiffening breeze.

Climbing slush-frosted snow, we move slowly like the departing storm. Out of the blue I say, "Do you remember the 'bears' that night in Georgia on the Appalachian Trail?"

"My *imaginary* bears?" you laugh. "I really thought that I could fight them off with my hiking poles."

I decide not to point out the day-old grizzly bear scat that blackens a depression in the snow. We are not alone, but I don't want to alarm you.

Shafts of sunlight shine like laser beams on the Divide's crags and battlements. The remnants of the hailstorm continue to push east toward the Great Plains.

At Brown Pass, a rainbow splashes color on the blue-black buttes. The geometry of space and void—clouds and mountains—is replicated in our own expansive feelings. Soaked on the outside but glowing inside, we are exactly where we want to be.

Tine, there is an unexpected continuity between my decades on the trail and our life together. Both involve exploration, but you have helped me to reach a new level of contentment. We are mutual pathfinders. No matter where life takes us, we will be on the right trail if we are together.

Books from My Backpack

BECAUSE THE NEXT best thing to hiking is reading about it, I am always looking for outstanding walk narratives. In 1988 I anthologized seventy-seven gems in *Shank's Mare: A Compendium of Remarkable Walks*. I confess that I often selected those passages partly for their sheer enthusiasm. As I wrote then, "Voluntary walking is not a rejection of technology as much as it is a reaffirmation of the pleasure of having two legs ... Watch out! By the time you finish this book you will be as restless as I am today. And foot powders can't cure *this* itch."

1988 seems like ancient history because we, a quarter century later, are in the midst of an explosion of hiker literature. Leaving aside relatively recent venues such as blogs and Web sites, the intervening years have seen an amazing proliferation of book titles. Lon Chenowith published *Five Million Steps*, Wilson Brandon weighed in at *Seven Million Steps*, and Nimblewill Nomad strode into print with *Ten Million Steps*. What could possibly be next?

Undaunted, I wish to use this chapter to showcase an entirely new crop of post-*Shank's Mare* books (whose publishing details are given in the Bibliography). I have chosen them with as much care as I would devote to finding a backcountry companion. Though their selection reflects my personal tastes and enthusiasms, my goal is to pay homage to the fast-evolving genre's diversity and richness. I make no pretense that this is a definitive list. All I can say is that I have selected these books to meet a tough test: that each must deserve a place in my knapsack. For an ounce-conscious hiker, that is the ultimate standard.

The Places in Between

For my first category—classic, international exploration—I have sought a contemporary incarnation of the over-the-top courageousness of such nineteenth-century explorers as Richard Francis

Burton and John Hanning Speke. Candidates include Englishman George Meegan's *The Longest Walk* (1988), a seven-year, 19,019-mile exploration of the Americas. There's also Ohioan Steven Newman's *Worldwalk* (1989), the record of his four-year round-the-world adventure. That was a walk in the park compared to Englishwoman Ffyona Campbell's *The Whole Story* (1996), an eleven-year, 20,000-mile foot-powered circumnavigation of the earth. Yet for sheer gutsiness it's hard to top Englishman Ranulph Fiennes's *Mind Over Matter* (1993), his 1,350-mile, unsupported crossing of the Antarctic continent.

However, I've selected *The Places in Between* (2006), a guaranteed-admission-to-the-Explorers-Club adventure from the inestimable Scotsman Rory Stewart (1973–). Six weeks after the defeat of the Taliban, he trekked across Afghanistan with both literary flair and admirable sang froid. I feel much the better for his courage and perseverance. There is nothing flashy or confessional about Stewart: just a hero who used his wits to navigate political and physical hardships with elan and style. After innumerable grueling trials, he eventually developed an admirable Zen perspective. "I began to count my breaths and my steps," he wrote, "and to recite phrases to myself, pushing thoughts away." Through such meditation he discovered a hitherto-unknown serenity. "It was," he said, "what I valued most about walking."

Part adventure, part anthropology, *The Places in Between* drew me forward in the society-in-rapid-transition manner of Patrick Leigh Fermor's classic account of his 1933 walk across Europe. Like Fermor, Stewart displays brio, courage, and erudition that will never go out of style.

High Summer: Backpacking the Canadian Rockies

There are some people who cannot resist a challenge. The indefatigable Scottish adventurer Chris Townsend (1949–) had an epiphany when he learned from *The Handbook of the Canadian Rockies* that no one had yet end-to-ended the 1,450-kilometer length of that vast mountain chain. "I felt a thrill of excitement ... and knew instantly that I would take up the challenge." The result was *High Summer: Backpacking the Canadian Rockies* (1989). I was impressed by the author's equanimity in the face of malevolent brush, bad maps, and nasty weather. The northern half of his 1,600-mile, four-month trip involved genuine exploration. Across steep canyons and wild rivers, Chris Townsend overcame exhaustion and misturns. As our mutual Yorkshire friend, John Manning, says: "Chris's writing focuses so closely on the backpacking that he transports you to the Rockies, evokes memories of trails you've hiked in the past, and inspires you to look for new, more adventurous trails to follow."

Ultimately I recommend *High Summer* because I like Chris Townsend's attitude:

> *To reach the end is not the reason for making such a trek. Whilst having a goal helps to keep me going when I'm tired or the weather is bad, the real reason for such a walk is to live in the wilderness for a long enough period to feel at home there, to feel part of the natural world. That's why I usually go on my own: such a feeling being much harder to achieve when in the company, however congenial, of others.*

This is not self-revelatory, confessional prose. But if you yearn for a good old-fashioned slog across months of nasty brush, this book is for you.

A Blistered Kind of Love: One Couple's Trial by Trail

This book differs dramatically from Rory Stewart's and from Chris Townsend's. Those two stalwart Scots were exposed to so much daily danger that their hikes were essentially high-wire balancing acts without a safety net. When twenty-somethings Angela and Duffy, on the other hand, thru-hiked the well-marked, luxuriously graded Pacific Crest Trail in 2000, their challenges were, shall we say, more pedestrian. For instance, one afternoon they went astray in the Sierra. To regain the PCT they were obliged to bivouac off-piste. Angela wrote, "I think I can safely say that no one had ever camped in that exact spot before, but while I could appreciate the beauty of our pristine surroundings, being so far off-course overnight made me nervous." When she and Duffy found the trail the next morning, "he fell to his knees and kissed the tread."

Obviously we readers are in very different company with this pair than with our two laconic Scots. But—and this is a big *but*—that does not detract at all from the value of Angela and Duffy's narrative. For here is the essential thing about hiking: it is not competitive so much as it is personal.

My trail mantra is *hike your own hike* because life is altogether too full of beat-the-clock striving. Sensible hikers resist the urge to measure themselves against other people's times and mileages. In the case of Angela and Duffy, their "pilgrimage was all about discovering America, nature, and ourselves (not necessarily in that order)." A *Blistered Kind of Love* (2003) consists of alternating chapters from each of their perspectives.

As the lovers inched their way northward, they evolved as a couple. At first, Angela worried so much that her head ached as much as her feet. She fretted about everything from her credit card bill to whether she was making her parents sad to whether she was or was not a good person. Despite her worrywart introspection, she did discover that rarest of joys, romance:

> *The romance was in what we accomplished together.*
> *Climbing Mount Whitney, the tallest mountain in the*
> *contiguous U.S.; helping one another through thirty-mile*
> *days; holding hands across ice, snow, as well as treacherous*
> *fords, and knowing limb—if not life—depended on our grip;*
> *even carrying a little extra weight when the other person*
> *was hurting. These and other situations created a bond and*
> *partnership that candlelight dinners and strolls on the beach*
> *couldn't match.*

Ultimately I recommend *A Blistered Kind of Love* not only for its fine evocation of the PCT but also for its sensitive understanding of what it takes to be a couple. Read it if you believe (or want to believe) in romantic love.

Zero Days: The Real-life Adventure of Captain Bligh, Nellie Bly, and 10-year-old Scrambler on the Pacific Coast Trail

Only a brave soul would embark afoot on a long journey with one or more young children. But that is what Dervla Murphy did in *Eight Feet in the Andes* (1983), the story of her 1,300-mile mule-assisted walk through the Peruvian Andes. With great good humor she recounted hers and her daughter's travails among some of the world's most spectacular mountains. Enough other moms have followed suit that we have the makings of a parenting-on-foot genre. Spud Talbot-Ponsonby in *Small Steps with Heavy Hooves* (1998) took her sixteen-month-old son on a trek across northeast Scotland. Cindy Ross in *Scraping Heaven* (2003) described her family's five-summer, 3,100-mile llama trek on the Continental Divide Trail.

Societal stresses and financial pressures often place a severe strain on families' cohesion and love. Against that bleak reality, I was cheered by Barbara Egbert's *Zero Days* (2008), in which she recounts the thru-hike of the Pacific Coast Trail that she undertook with her husband and their ten-year-old daughter. I personally know few children (or parents) who would willingly spend 137 nights together in a 6-by-8-foot tent. Barbara explained it this way:

> *Sometimes we were so much on the outs with each other, I thought we'd never be on speaking terms again. But we've always been a close family, and it was that willingness to stay close, no matter how badly we wanted to divorce and disown each other, that formed us into a group capable of taking on almost any challenge.*

I pulled down 1,500 miles on the PCT during that same summer (2004) when the Egberts went border to border. As an adult, I can attest to the difficulties that ten-year-old Scrambler faced. Her physical feat earns my applause but her mother's book wins my kudos for its inspired depiction of familial possibilities. *Zero Days* reminded me of the potential richness and harmoniousness of family relationships.

Walking to Vermont

If you are less interested in children than retirees, I suggest that you read *A Walk Across France* (1992). Upon resigning at age forty-five from his career on Wall Street, author Miles Moreland set out with his wife to walk from the Mediterranean to the Atlantic via quaint towns, cheery cafes, and ripening vineyards. I loved it.

More recently, sixty-five-year-old Christopher Wren's shopping maven of a wife didn't accompany him on his hike. She did, however, make a few expensive cameo appearances in *Walking To Vermont* (2004) that helped me to understand the extent of the author's hesitant transition from conventional middle-class respectability. At first on the way north from New York City, "grungy and unshaven," he felt "awkward to rub shoulders with ordinary tourists." He began with a jaundiced view of the Appalachian Trail's thru-hikers. "Probe deeply enough," he wrote, "and you'll find travelers who are between jobs, marriages, schools, or bad checks. They are walking toward emotional or spiritual fulfillment or away from stress and worse problems they don't want to talk about." By the time his trip was over he had loosened up enough to do thru-hikerly things such as skinny dip in ponds and yogi for fresh-baked cookies. Once two thrus, total strangers, slowed their pace enough to permit him to reach Mount Greylock's Bascom Lodge with them in time for dinner. Astonished, he wrote, "I have not done as much for some people I knew better, or had them do as much for me."

Each year publishers release a new slew of trail journals. The best authors portray their passion within a social and/ or historical context. I admire the way that Christopher Wren, retired international correspondent, focused his overseas-honed reportorial skills on the American recreational trail experience. In story after story, he reminded me that hiker's problems are innocuous compared to Third World poverty and violence.

What I like even more about *Walking to Vermont* is that Wren came to understand that his five-week, 400-mile journey mattered more than its completion. He said, "[T]he best part was discovering that I had not really finished, because walking to Vermont turned out to be about a state of mind."

At any age—but perhaps especially after retirement—walking can supply both equanimity and a sense of purpose. Anyone can have his or her own version of a walk to Vermont. The opportunity is always out there, waiting.

Wandering Home: A Long Walk across America's Most Hopeful Landscape: Vermont's Champlain Valley and New York's Adirondacks

It should be no surprise that long-distance writers sometimes produce environmental manifestos. For instance, Gary Ferguson's 1993 *Walking down the Wild* is as much about eco-politics as it is about his 500-mile Yellowstone trek. Similarly Bill McKibben's *Wandering Home* (2005) is about the future of the vast area between the heights of Vermont's Green Mountains and the peaks of the Adirondack Mountains. (I confess that I'm partly recommending it because its subject, a stroll from Vermont's Green Mountains to the heart of New York's Adirondacks, roughly follows part of my proposed transcontinental Sea-To-Sea Route.)

Long ago McKibben (1960–) fell in love with "these yellow birches, the bear who left that berry-filled pile of scat, those particular loons laughing on this particular lake." He writes, "I have the great good fortune to have found the place I was supposed to inhabit, a place in whose largeness I can sense the whole world but yet is small enough for me to comprehend."

Wandering Home is an on-foot paean to the land and its people. I admire Bill McKibben for his willingness to use oral history to ferret out traditional values that most conservationists ignore. I delight in his recognition of the return of New England's forests as something elemental and unplanned. I recommend this and his other books' portrayal of community, wildness, and sustainability. Reading Bill McKibben made me smile.

Honorable Bandit: A Walk across Corsica

In writing about his two-week traverse of Corsica on GR20, Brian Bouldrey wanted to explain "why it is that I spend so much of my spare time with a backpack strapped over my shoulders ... and why others might do it, too." His *Honorable Bandit* (2007) is a stream-of-consciousness riff that emulates the seemingly aimless chatter that ricochets around in our heads as we walk. He says, "Walking is a back-to-nature business, but it also conjures a moving city full of secondary Dickensian grotesques, or the long scrollwork line of figures decorating an Egyptian wall, or a Greek vase, coming to me single file, every one of them with a posture or antic or good joke to tell."

Having long wanted to hike the trans-Corsica trail, I found that doing so vicariously with Brian Bouldrey was like walking into the foreign terrain of someone else's head. It was "Hike your own trail" on steroids. Halfway into his two-week hike, he says, "Each day was so challenging I can barely manage thinking about going on for another week. These frightening climbs up mountain peaks, lifting myself up thousands of feet over boulders and then slogging down through loose scree and whatever else is on the trail—how long can this go on?"

I admire this book for it frank exploration of motivations. The author described his 1989 Castro District wedding to his AIDS-doomed partner Jeff. "I slipped a ring onto Jeff's hands, gnarled with runaway warts and staph (opportunistic!) infections." After a haze of "end-of-the-world parties" between 1988 and 1993, when his coterie perished one by one, Bouldrey literally walked away and has been walking ever since.

I am always very curious to know why inveterate walkers do what they do. *Honorable Bandit* is the most sustained and thorough explanation that I have ever read.

Wanderlust: A History of Walking

Rebecca Solnit (1961–) is a polymath of prodigious proportions. Her *Wanderlust* (2000) spans the centuries to describe a fine panoply of walkers from sexworkers (street walkers) to boulvardiers to mountaineers. She easily jumps from landscape aesthetics to railway history in order to put pedestrianism into perspective. Who else but this fine essayist could write, "If there was a golden age of walking, it arose from a desire to travel through the open spaces of the world unarmored by vehicles, unafraid to mingle with different kinds of people."

"Walking as a cultural activity, as a pleasure, as travel, as a way of getting around, is fading," she writes, "and with it goes an ancient and profound relationship between body, world, and imagination ... Walking is an indicator species for various kinds of freedoms and pleasures: free time, free and alluring space, and unhindered bodies."

Non-walkers often assume that journeying on foot must be boring. Solnit knows better: that a large part of perambulation is cogitation. As she puts it, "Exploring the world is one of the best ways of exploring the mind, and walking travels both terrains."

I enjoyed reading Solnit's *Wanderlust* in conjunction with her *A Field Guide to Getting Lost* (2005). Part of the reason that I love walking is its opportunity to lose myself in the vast Other. She expresses it this way: "Leave the door open for the unknown, the door into the dark. That's where the most important things come from, where you yourself came from, and where you will go."

When both my mind and body are on the march, I free associate everything from the cactus 20 feet ahead to a snippet of childhood conversation to tomorrow's gutbuster pigout. Reading Rebecca Solnit is similarly liberating.

As Far as the Eye Can See: Reflections of an Appalachian Trail Hiker

About twenty years ago a young father (1955–) looked back on an end-to-end hike he'd taken a decade earlier when he'd been twenty-three. The result was David Brill's *As Far as the Eye Can See* (1990). Unlike other books in the crowded thru-hike genre, this one was arranged thematically, not chronologically. Its chapters were: Fear; Learning to Walk, Learning to See; Seasons; Our Gang; Linear Community; Bad Company; Wasted Along the Way; Gear; Stopping Along the Way; Hot Springs Rhapsody; Critters; Where I Live; Special Attractions; and Coming Home. Those prosaic titles faithfully suggest Brill's subject matter but fail to indicate the thoughtful nature of his writing. Here is a sample:

> *From weeks of living out of a thirty-five pound pack, I learned to find contentment in simple things and to rely on myself and my resources to surmount obstacles. From long days spent tromping through rain and cold, I learned that whenever I felt beaten, spent, exhausted, and ready to quit, there was always something left and that if I delved deep enough, I could always find the strength to keep moving forward. From watching the seasons yield one to the next, daylight surrender to night, and darkness give way to morning, I discovered that in the midst of chaos order and purpose are present for us. From the unqualified kindness shared among travelers in the backcountry, I learned that for all the cruelty loose in the world, people care deeply for their fellow creatures. And I learned that whenever I lose sight of those lessons, I can regain them by returning to the trail.*

Authenticity is the central characteristic of good trail writing. We want to know without a doubt that the author walked his or her walk. We want to feel comfortable exploring and learning with him or her. For my money David Brill (AT 1979, PNT 1981) is one of the most poetic and simpatico celebrants of the trail experience.

A Walk in the Woods:
Rediscovering America on the Appalachian Trail

David Miller's *Awol on the Appalachian Trail* (2006) and Lawrence Alexander's *Through Hiker's Eyes* (2008) are some of the best written of the annual flood of new entrants in the thru-hiker literature. However, none of the many contenders have yet dethroned Bill Bryson's *A Walk in the Woods* (1998) as the most successful recent attempt to showcase hiking for a mass audience.

Just as Colin Fletcher was the celebrity hiker of the 1960s and Eric Ryback and Peter Jenkins were his 1970s equivalents, Bill Bryson (1951–) still occupies that niche today. If I ask strangers if they know anything about hiking, they often mention having read *A Walk in the Woods*. Its popularity is also apparent on Amazon's Web site, where many reviewers report that their disinterest in hiking was overcome by Bryson's humorous tale of two middle-aged nitwits loose on the Appalachian Trail.

Because the Sad Sack pair only managed to hike about a third of the fourteen-state, 2,175-mile AT, the book developed a bad reputation, at least initially, among thru-hikers. My own reaction then and now is that Bryson makes fun of everything I hold dear, but he does it in such a sidesplittingly funny way that I wish there were a hundred more writers like him to charm non-hikers into giving walking a try. For many, many months his saga strode across the *New York Times* bestseller list with its uplifting message disguised as humor:

I learned to pitch a tent and sleep beneath the stars. For
a brief, proud period I was slender and fit. I gained a
profound respect for wilderness and nature and the benign

dark power of woods. I understand now, in a way I never did before, the colossal scale of the world. I found patience and fortitude that I didn't know I had. I discovered an America that millions of people scarcely know exists. I made a friend. I came home.

More than a decade after its publication, what stands out about *A Walk*? Its admirers universally say that they remember the funny bits about Bryson's and his companion Katz's ineptness. However, in rereading the book now, I see that it is tricked out with long expository passages about environmental policy and trail history. Having attempted that sleight of hand myself, I am in awe of anyone who can sugarcoat such seemingly indigestible roughage for sedentary Americans.

My ten-book list ends with *A Walk in the Woods* because of Bryson's proven ability to proselytize non-walkers. He and Katz remind us that we do not need to be capable of crossing Antarctica to enjoy walking. The fun is waiting for us right now at the nearest trailhead.

Who will be tomorrow's Bryson? So far no *flâneur* or thru-hiker has taken the twenty-first-century's reading public by storm. Where is our Fletcher [*The Man Who Walked Through Time*] or our Jenkins [*A Walk Across America*]? What undiscovered author will sashay onto the bestseller lists? Will it be, say, a mother who describes her family's adventures on the East Coast Greenway or an unemployed investment banker who finds redemption on the Sea-To-Sea Route? I hope that she is muddying her boots right now or possibly even thinking up her book's first sentence.

Mystery hiker: whoever you are, I and many other people are eager to read what you have to say.

Hiking's Enduring Appeal

*Aloha, everyone. So today is my last day at work. They got
me a cake and some gag gifts (suction cup bow and arrow
and a bug net). Now I just have to go to my party, finish
packing, and pay a few last bills (speeding ticket). The
excitement has been causing insomnia. I can't wait to start
this trail I've been dreaming and planning for all this time.
Peace.*

Junaid Dawud, Pacific Crest Trail, 4-13-06

I STRODE FORWARD, hoping to emerge onto the primeval shore
from the Olympic Peninsula's temperate rain forest. After miles
of mosses, ferns, salal, Oregon grape, and false Solomon's seal,
I finally sensed a low rumble up ahead where the fir and spruce
thinned out. Soon there was no mistaking the sound of waves
throwing themselves upon the western edge of the continent.

From the top of the embankment, my inland eyes gorged on
gleaming expanses of sand, water, and islands. Breaking free of
the last nettles and alders, I scrambled over huge driftwood logs to
reach the wet, glorious sand.

After so long in the quiet forest, I felt engulfed by the coast's
wild cacophony. Breakers backed and filled; birds mewed and
squawked. I squinted at spume glistening in the radiant light.
Wherever I looked, the evolutionary play of natural forces shone
forth in the flight of wings, the shapes of seashells, and the diversity
of tide pools.

I became a beachcomber among the rubber duckies, sand-filled
gloves, and sorry sneakers that had arrived here from across the
globe via oceanic circulation systems. When my luck turned up an
actual note in a bottle, I thought I had hit the Robinson Crusoe
jackpot. A month later I contacted Lore Geither, who replied from
Herman's Delicatessen in San Francisco. "I was on a German

freighter with nothing else to do," she wrote, "so I dropped some bottles with silly notes in them between San Francisco and Vancouver. If you ever come to San Francisco, look me up."

THE NEXT MORNING after Cygnus the Swan sank low on the horizon, I awoke to the distant sounds of low tide. They reminded me that I was about to live by the predictable rhythms of the moon's gravitational pull. Out came my tide chart. I would need it to avoid becoming trapped at the base of some impassable wave-smashed headland.

Walking beside the ocean was so full of incidents, large and small, that it upended my concept of time. Even minutes seemed fuller on the coast.

I had already forgotten how much I had loved the rain forest when Goodman Creek's reefs and cliffs forced me to take a short detour inland through an extravagant mix of devil's club, mosses, salmonberry, ferns, elderberries, and cow parsnips. The strong cadences of the sea gave way to the mossy silences of the deep woods. From the coast's broad horizon, my gaze narrowed to giant slugs and seedling-festooned stumps.

Half an hour later, atop an alder bluff, I popped out of the forest in time to witness a whirling kaleidoscope of gulls whose cries were half drowned out by the thunder of the rising tide. Surf scoters swam and dove in the calmer water behind the breakers. A half-dozen cormorants dried their crucifix-like wings while others sped low over the ocean's surface. A great blue heron waited expectantly. Oystercatchers probed dark strands of finger kelp with their gleaming, orange bills. The restless energy of sandpipers mimicked the rising, breaking, and falling of the sea.

Thermal billows draped the sky in a magnificent echo of the vegetation that decorated offshore seastacks. In breeding season, the air above such islands resembles a swarm of midges as seabirds by the hundreds of thousands fly to and from their nests.

At a silver sea flecked with reefs and islands, pelicans noisily roiled the water in pursuit of small fish. Others soared high above the melee before plunging into the backlit, pewter surface. They rarely surfaced without a fish in their fleshy pouches, leaving gulls to skirmish noisily for leftover scraps.

IN THAT WILD VISTA of sky and sand, of sea and island, I felt momentarily guilty to trod on so many limpets, whelks, and barnacles. But I was soon distracted by the scuttling frenzy of rock and shore crabs and by the playful antics of sea otters. The latter's crustacean-filled scat was so ubiquitous on little prominences that I wondered if the otters loved the coast's bold views as much as I did.

My first night north from La Push, I found enough washed-up unopened beer cans to fuel an epic orgy. But, not being much of drinker, I reveled instead in the sun's inch-by-inch disappearance over the horizon. I fell asleep watching gulls stand feet awash in a surging freshwater creek.

MORNING DAWNED OVERCAST and troubled. I felt a sea change in the air. Gulls now stood one-legged, facing south into the wind. Solitary shags arrowed down the coast.

I was so reluctant to break what I knew would be my last camp that I didn't get going until mean low tide at 10:00 a.m. According to the chart, that meant that I might not be able to complete the next six miles before the rising tide stopped me at the trip's last obstacle.

Endless ankle-breaking cobbles added to the lassitude that I felt; I did not want the trip to end. Sometimes I walked far out on the slippery, kelp-covered rocks. At other times, when the shortest line between two points was beside sheer bluffs, my gait resembled that of an Oregon rock crab.

Eventually the waves—which had once seemed so distant— began to thunder nearby under the force of freshened winds. The joys of rock hopping had worn so thin that I was glad to reach the eroded bluffs of a fine, sandy bay. *Easy going*, I thought—just before the afternoon's heavy mists precipitated into a light drizzle.

Greatly relieved to be off the rocks, I redoubled my effort to reach Cape Alava by nightfall. The grand crescent of that fine bay was some of the best walking I had yet seen. However, the closer I got to what I expected to be an easily crossed channel, the more formidable it looked. Soon two hundred feet of frothing, surging whitewater separated me from the next headland's spray-tossed ledges. Bare sand an hour or two earlier, that cramped angle of beach now roared with the energy of waves that had come thousands of miles across the open Pacific.

My tardy evening arrival coincided with the onset of a squall. After quickly setting up my tent, I napped into memories of the sound of all the limpets and whelks that I had crushed.

Sundown had already come and gone by the time I'd broken camp and was edging along the base of a slimy cliff to the entrance to a small tunnel. To make up for lost time I decided to use its underground passageway to shortcut the next little point. Though the entrance was only a few feet above the foaming, hissing breakers, I didn't hesitate. On hands and knees—pack grating on the ceiling—I inched my way into the dank hole. Fighting thoughts of being buried alive, I resisted the fear that lived in that raw prison. My knees ached from the pain of clambering toward the tunnel's faint outlet.

Popping out onto a murky keyhole beach, I clunked along the echoing cobbles. Happy to be free of the claustrophobic cave, I climbed up a notch at the far side into the welcoming scent of grass and fir.

The rain had stopped. A universe of stars shone in the wake of the squall. As I followed Polaris's wet reflection northward between the rain forest and the ocean, every faint glimmer of light had fallen underfoot. Rocks, far and few between, were as indistinct as a remembered mirage.

A friendly wind propelled me north over the tideflats. In the lee of my pack, I sailed along, following the barest outline of treetops that rose and fell with the undulations of the land. That breeze never blew from exactly the same quarter. As it feinted and jibed, I felt a changing mix of land warmth and ocean chill.

Up the trackless coast I sped with bounding steps and soaring spirits. Kelp and spruce perfumed the night. Ahead and behind, the glassy expanse of beach faded into nothingness. I was alone with the ceaseless movements of the sea and with the steady force of my gait.

Intoxicated by movement and starlight, I remembered my long-dreamed goal of creating a 1,200-mile path east to the Continental Divide. I shrugged, unwilling to be distracted from the heart-pounding joy of living in the moment.

On that phantom coast, I had walked a succession of sandy beaches, headland trails, wave-cut terraces, and low-tide wonder-lands. Accompanied by only the ocean's rises and ebbs. I'd been at home where the planet's rhythms were timeless and unbroken.

To feel so alive and so connected to Nature was a gift.

To want to provide it for others was my calling.

Glossary

Although hiking can be as simple as putting one foot in front of the other, the farther a person travels along that trail the more he or she will encounter its specialized vocabulary. Knowing the correct words and phrases is part of the fun.

Base weight: a full pack's weight minus food, water, and fuel.

Big Miles: significant daily mileage hiked on a long-distance trail.

Blue blazing: taking shortcuts on side trails that are marked with blue blazes.

Bonus Miles: extra walking above and beyond a trail's actual length (as in side trips to and from resupply points).

Bounce box: a container of things that a thru-hiker may want to use at stops throughout the course of a long hike. A bounce box is usually mailed ahead to the next stop where it will be needed.

Flipfloppers: thru-hikers who leapfrog along the trail by mixing the order of the sections that they hike.

Food drop: a box of supplies that will be consumed during part of a long hike. Hikers often mail their food drops to themselves care of General Delivery at one or more post offices near the trail.

Gutbuster: an all-you-can-eat pigout.

Homestay: overnight lodging (often unexpected) in someone's home.

Nero: an almost zero-miles day.

NoBos: northbound thrus.

Pulaski: a chopping and trenching tool commonly used by trailbuilders and firefighters.

Pull down (v.): to walk a certain distance per day, as in, "I pulled down 25 today."

Slackpacker: a hiker whose pack is carried by someone else (usually in a vehicle).

Sobos: southbound thrus.

Snoose: chewing tobacco (not a hiker term).

Thru-hiker: someone who hikes a major portion of or the entirety of a long-distance trail straight through. Thru-hikers (or thrus) are also sometimes called end-to-enders.

Trail angels: Good Samaritans who help hikers by doing such things as providing lodging, food, water, or trailhead rides.

Trail magic: serendipitous good fortune.

Triple Crown: the Appalachian Trail, Pacific Crest Trail, and Continental Divide Trail.

Wave, the: hikers who progress more or less *en masse* toward the terminus of a long-distance trail. As in (regarding the AT), "The Wave from Springer Mountain in Georgia has already reached Damascus, Virginia."

Yellow blazing: skipping part of a trail by hitchiking.

Yogi (v.): to beg for rides, food, etc. (in the manner of Yogi Bear).

Zero (day): a rest day, usually in a trail town, as in, "I took four zeroes in Shasta City to give my feet a break."

Notes

INTRODUCTION

"Pathfinder grew out of my experiences": Terry Wood, "A Trail not for the Faint of Foot," *Seattle Times*, May 3, 2001, book review.

I BECAME A HIKER

"I became a hiker because": Walters thru-hiked the Cascade Crest Trail with Earl Shaffer in 1962. In 1948, when he was twenty-nine, Earl had been the first person ever to thru-hike the Appalachian Trail.

"Because I was content": Ralph Waldo Emerson, "Musketaquid," *Early Poems of Ralph Waldo Emerson*. (New York: Thomas Y. Crowell & Company, 1899).

THE BAD BOYS

"In America's recreational trails world": As of 2011, America still has only eleven (dating from between 1968 and 2009).

"I was such a complete outsider": James E. Lalonde, "The Ultimate Northwest Trail: Is Longer Necessarily Better?" *The Weekly*, August 4-10, 1976. James E. Lalonde, "A Supertrail In Trouble," *The Weekly*, April 26-May 2, 1978.

"I should have anticipated": Eric Ryback. *The High Adventure of Eric Ryback: Canada to Mexico on Foot*. (San Francisco, CA: Chronicle Books, 1971.)

"However, Seattle's Old Guard": Barney "Scout" Mann, "Ryback Returns: The Youngster Who Put the PCT on the Map in 1970 Surfaces to Pay Homage at Monument 252, the Obscure Place Where History Was Made," *PCT Communicator*, September, 2009.

"As has been shown by the example": "N3C Board Takes Stand on Trail Proposal," *The Wild Cascades*, Spring 1977, 11.

"My buddy, Port of Seattle": Dee Molenaar, *The Challenge of Rainier: A Record of the Exploration and Ascents, Triumphs and Tragedies, on the Northwest's Greatest Mountain* (Seattle, WA: The Mountaineers Books, 3rd ed. 1979), 149. "Camp Schurman is the name given to the shelter cabin constructed by volunteer labor of many mountaineers and Explorer Scouts headed by veteran Mountain Rescue men John Simac, Max Eckenburg, Ome Daiber, and Bill Butler. The first two or three summers of the project involved backpacking heavy steel culvert sections, lumber, and other construction materials from White River Campground to the Prow. I will long remember the Big Carry as it started in 1958, scores of climbers and hikers of all ages and walks of life, old climbers and young Scouts, Mountain Rescue personnel, ex-Park rangers and one-time summit guides. The cabin was eventually completed after several more summers of hard work."

RALPH THAYER'S BROADAXE

"At the beginning of the 1978": Ralph Thayer's oral history is included in the Lexikos edition (New York: Paragon House, 1990) of my book *River Pigs and Cayuses*, pp. 107-12.

"I genuinely wanted Ralph Thayer's advice": *River Pigs and Cayuses*, p xvi.

MURDER MYSTERY

"Long a mecca for backcountry conviviality": Read more about Paul Louden in *River Pigs and Cayuses*, pp. 126-32.

"I interviewed Paul": These gentlemen, now deceased, were all volunteer Tungsten Mine maintainers, a role now discouraged by misguided Forest Service administrators. I urge the government to preserve this important piece of public heritage.

THE OKANOGAN

"There was the greatest commotion": Richard F. Steele, *History of North Washington: An Illustrated History of Stevens, Ferry, Okanogan and Chelan Counties.* (Spokane, WA: Western Historical Publishing Company, 1904), 407.

TRAIL MAGIC

"After William's story": Ron Strickland, *Whistlepunks and Geoducks: Oral Histories from the Pacific Northwest.* (New York, NY: Paragon House, 1990), 205-11.

LONGING FOR ROOTS

"Frustration levels were rising": Rick Bass, *Winter: Notes from Montana* (Boston, MA: Houghton Mifflin/Seymour Lawrence, 1991), 8.

"Sherrie and Scott were a fresh-scrubbed pair": Rick Bass, *Why I Came West* (Boston, MA: Houghton Mifflin, 2008), 161.

"I would have been much more convinced": Rick Bass, *The Deer Pasture* (College Station, TX: Texas A & M University Press, 1985).

"That was the essence of the situation": Rick Bass, *Why I Came West* (Boston, MA: Houghton Mifflin, 2008), 152.

SOLO

"I had undergone a serious transformation": Eric Ryback, *The High Adventure of Eric Ryback: Canada to Mexico on Foot* (San Francisco, CA: Chronicle Books, 1971), 188.

"A solo hike may be just the thing": Cindy Ross and Todd Gladfelter, *A Hiker's Companion: 12,000 Miles of Trail-Tested Wisdom* (Seattle: The Mountaineers, 1993), 111.

"The PNT trip was really something": Reid Cross, letter to the author, August 21, 1975.

"Don't hike alone": Francis Tapon, e-mail to the author, January 21, 2010.

SELKIRK MOUNTAINS

"From Lower Ball Lake": Ron Strickland, *Pacific Northwest Trail Guide* (Seattle, WA: The Writing Works, 1984), 86.

"I was overjoyed to have found": Laura and Guy Waterman, *Forest and Crag: A History of Hiking, Trail Blazing, and Adventure in the Northeast Mountains* (Boston, MA: Appalachian Mountain Club, 1989), 223.

PASS IT ON

footnote: Ron Strickland. *Pacific Northwest Trail Guide.* (Seattle, WA: The Writing Works, 1984.)

"I very much enjoyed": Harvey Manning, letter to the author, April 8, 1971.

"What he no doubt meant": Harvey Manning, letter to the author, June 11, 1971; March 4, 1972.

"I credit my father and my Boy Scout Troop": Brian Robinson, e-mail to the author, June 6, 2008.

"Brian's father, Roy": Roy Robinson, e-mail to the author, June 27, 2008.

"My own latest dream": Ron Strickland, "Ocean to Ocean!" *The Nor'wester*, vol. XVIII nos. 3 & 4, summer/autumn 1996.

"My attempt to extrapolate": Peter Flax, "Sea to Shining Sea," *Backpacker Magazine*, v. 31, no. 210, February 2003.

"Conquering the [C2C] route alone": David Howard, "Person of the Year: Andrew Skurka, Tireless Thru-hiker Goes the Distance—and Then Some," *Backpacker Magazine*, August 2005, 65.

"Andrew subsequently described his adventures": Daniel Duane, "2007 Adventurer of the Year: The Walking Man," *National Geographic Adventure*, December 2007/January 2008, 87.

"He came in just at dusk": Kay Kujawa, e-mail to author, September 18, 2008.

"That was also the reaction": Kirt Stage-Harvey, e-mail to author,
    September 8, 2008.
"We were so fascinated by Andy's adventure": Kay Kujawa, e-mail
    to author, September 18, 2008.
"At first I was not in favor": Karen Skurka, e-mail to author,
    September 2, 2008.

THE PURCELL MOUNTAINS
"When I first explored the Purcell Mountains": Ron Strickland,
    River Pigs and Cayuses (Corvallis: Oregon State University Press,
    2001), 89-92.

"A LABOR OF TRULY OBSESSIVE LOVE"
"As a lover of guidebooks": Terry Wood, "A Trail not for the Faint
    of Foot," *Seattle Times*, May 3, 2001, book review. "The newly
    released second edition arrives more than 30 years after Strickland
    was smitten by the fanciful idea. Considerable grass-roots effort—
    much of it Strickland's—has been devoted to nursing the trail
    from concept to reality. After three decades, the trail remains, he
    acknowledges, a work in progress, 'an informally bound skein of
    existing trails, backcountry roads, Indian routes, stock driveways
    and cross-country travel.' Think you want to tackle the whole
    route? Be forewarned, he writes: 'You are going to have to work
    to enjoy the Pacific Northwest Trail.'"
"He was angry at me, too": Harvey Manning, letter to the author,
    July 12, 2001.
"Jeffrey Schaffer (1943–) wrote most": He described about 1,570
    miles of the PCT's 2,650-mile total.
"One day in 1972, I saw": Jeffrey P. Schaffer, e-mail to the author,
    April 25, 2008.
"Jeff's idiosyncracy was that his fascination": Jeffrey P. Schaffer, *The
    Pacific Crest Trail: Volume 2: Oregon and Washington* (Berkeley,
    CA: Wilderness Press, 1974), 102.
"Press onward, indeed!": Jeffrey P. Schaffer. *The Geomorphic
    Evolution of the Yosemite Valley and Sierra Nevada Landscapes:
    Solving the Riddles in the Rocks.* (Berkeley, CA: Wilderness Press,
    1997.)
"I am less pleased with Jeff's recent news": Jeffrey P. Schaffer, e-mail
    to the author, April 25, 2008.
"Dear Ron, This'll be quick": Harvey Manning, letter to the author,
    June 28, 1974.
"Harvey once described himself to me": *Walking the Beach to
    Bellingham* was reprinted by Oregon State University Press in its
    Northwest Reprints Series in 2002.

"I feel fortunate that e-mail didn't exist": Harvey Manning, letter to the author, December 11, 1971, and December 4, 1973.

"There was worse": Harvey Manning, letter to the author, February 17, 2003.

"Ai-yee, Ron! I've cast the old world": Harvey Manning, letter to author, December 26, 2000. His sign-off phrase is the title of a book by George Orwell.

"The appetite is as wild": Harvey Manning, letter to author, September 13, 1975.

"We are enjoying a glorious period": Jackie McDonnell, *Yogi's CDT Handbook: Planning Tips and Town Guide* (Shawnee Mission, KS: Yogi's Books, 2006). David Miller, *The A.T. Guide: A Handbook for Hiking the Appalachian Trail* (Titusville, FL: Jerelyn Press, 2010).

"Jackie McDonnell and David Miller had clever ideas": Of course, not all guidebooks are about long-distance trails. Many center around the needs of day hikers in particular areas. *Around Bend*, Scott Cook's excellent guide to day hiking around Bend, Oregon, is an informative, humorous, and well-organized example.

"WILLFUL AND ECCENTRIC"

"We want to build a fish pond": Robert Jay Mathews, personal interview, July 1, 1978.

"Bob Mathews died such an incredibly": Kevin Flynn and Gary Gerhardt, *The Silent Brotherhood: Inside America's Racist Underground* (New York: Signet, 1990), 382.

"He supposedly said, 'Do not go'": Prior to its 2009 designation by Congress it was known as the 3-M Trail, and was composed of (1) the Mattabesett Trail, (2) the Metacomet Trail, and (3) the Metacomet-Monadnock Trail. Laura and Guy Waterman, *Forest and Crag: A History of Hiking, Trail Blazing, and Adventure in the Northeast Mountains* (Boston, MA: Appalachian Mountain Club, 1989), 440, 436.

"In prewar titans such as Heermance": Laura and Guy Waterman, *Forest and Crag: A History of Hiking, Trail Blazing, and Adventure in the Northeast Mountains* (Boston, MA: Appalachian Mountain Club, 1989), 437.

"Professor Walter M. Banfield": Laura and Guy Waterman, *Forest and Crag: A History of Hiking, Trail Blazing, and Adventure in the Northeast Mountains* (Boston, MA: Appalachian Mountain Club, 1989), 615.

"I arrived in Guilford, Connecticut": Erik Lacitis, "A Journey of Thousands of Steps," *Seattle Times*, October 3, 2009.

"The lanky, narrow-boned man at my side": John Harlin, "The Prophet of the PNT," *Backpacker Magazine*, May 2000.

TEN ESSENTIALS

"I tell everyone to extend a little hospitality": Ollie Mae Wilson, letter to the author, September 17, 2008.

"In 2000, software development": Mark Samsel, e-mail to the author, January 28, 2010.

"In April 2004, Andrew Walters": Andrew Walters, e-mail to the author, January 29, 2010. Hillary Nelson, "When Is an ATV not an ATV?: When the State Decides It's Really a Snowmobile," *Concord Monitor*, March 9, 2008.

"TRAVELING LIGHT"

"At midnight I rose quietly": Walter Weston, *Mountaineering and Exploring in the Japanese Alps* (London, UK: John Murray, 1896), 26.

"threw away quite a number of things": Matsuo Basho. Nobuyuki Yuasa, translator. *The Narrow Road to the Deep North and Other Travel Sketches* (New York: Penguin books, 1966), 81.

"*Asa yū ni kiri*": Kumiko Harada, letter to the author, October 31, 2008.

THE PATH AHEAD

"The publishing industry may be headed": Self-published books, despite their poor reputation, can sometimes be quite excellent. For instance, I recommend Brandon Wilson's *Over the Top & Back Again* for memorable characters, funny incidents, and hearty trail fun.

"For many years I was mainly interested": Denny Nackoney, e-mail to the author, February 2, 2010.

"The solution is to create": Here is an example of a lack of standardization that still irks me. In 2009, regional officials of the Forest Service refused to allow the PNT to be marked with the customary paint and/or medallion blazes. My gripe is that they felt that they were under no obligation to adhere to the traditional, nationwide practice of blazing national scenic trails. How crazy is that?

BOOKS IN MY BACKPACK

"However, I've selected *The Places*": Rory Stewart, *The Places in Between* (New York: Harcourt, 2006), 76.

"To reach the end is not the reason": Chris Townsend, *High Summer: Backpacking the Canadian Rockies* (Seattle, WA: Cloudcap, 1989), 8.

"As the lovers inched their way": Angela and Duffy Ballard, *A Blistered Kind of Love: One Couple's Trial by Trail* (Seattle, WA: Mountaineers Books, 2003), 158.

"The romance was in what we accomplished": Ibid., 258.

"Sometimes we were so much on the outs": Barbara Egbert, *Zero Days: The Real-life Adventure of Captain Bligh, Nellie Bly, and 10-year-old Scrambler on the Pacific Crest Trail* (Berkeley, CA: Wilderness Press, 2008), 33.

"More recently, sixty-five-year-old": Christopher S. Wren, *Walking to Vermont: From Times Square into the Green Mountains—A Homeward Adventure* (New York: Simon and Schuster, 2004), 173.

"What I like even more": *Ibid.*, 351.

"Long ago McKibben": Bill McKibben, *Wandering Home: A Long Walk across America's Most Hopeful Landscape: Vermont's Champlain Valley and New York's Adirondacks* (New York: Crown, 2005), 157.

"In writing about his two-week traverse": Brian Bouldrey, *Honorable Bandit: A Walk across Corsica* (Madison, Wisconsin: Terrace Books, 2007), x.

"Rebecca Solnit (1961–) is a polymath": Rebecca Solnit. *Wanderlust: A History of Walking* (New York: Viking Penguin, 2000), 256.

"Non-walkers often assume": Ibid., 13.

"I enjoyed reading Solnit's *Wanderlust*": Rebecca Solnit, *A Field Guide to Getting Lost* (New York: Viking Penguin, 2005), 4.

"From weeks of living out of a thirty-five pound pack": David Brill, *As Far as the Eye Can See: Reflections of an Appalachian Trail Hiker*. 3rd ed. (Harpers Ferry, WV: Appalachian Trail Conservancy, 2004), 185.

"David Miller's *Awol on the Appalachian Trail*": Worldwide, Bryson's main bestselling competitor was Hape Kerkeling's 2006 *Ich Binn Dann Mal Weg: Meine Reise Auf Dem Jakobsweg* (translated into English in 2009 as *I'm Off Then: My Journey along the Camino De Santiago*).

"I learned to pitch a tent": Bill Bryson, *A Walk in the Woods* (New York: Broadway, 1998), 274.

WILDERNESS COAST

"I became a beachcomber": Curtis C. Ebbesmeyer, *Flotsametrics and the Floating World: How One Man's Obsession with Runaway Sneakers and Rubber Ducks Revolutionized Ocean Science* (New York: Smithsonian Books, 2009).

Bibliography

Walking always has the potential to make a good story. It has the advantage of a definite beginning and end. Life afoot is rich with possibility. Adventure calls.

Ron Strickland, Shank's Mare, 1988

For my most up-to-date bibliography of books about hiking please see: www.ronstrickland.com.

Adkins, Leonard M. *The Appalachian Trail: A Visitor's Companion.* Birmingham, AL: Menasha Ridge Press, 1998.
———. *Wildflowers of the Appalachian Trail.* 2nd ed. Birmingham, AL: Menasha Ridge Press, 2006.
Albers, Jan. *Hands on the Land: A History of the Vermont Landscape.* Cambridge, MA.: published for the Orton Family Foundation, Rutland, VT, by MIT Press, 2000. [See p. 259 for a photo of the "Three Musketeers," who were the first women to complete the Long Trail.]
Alcorn, Susan. *We're in the Mountains—Not Over the Hill: Tales and Tips from Seasoned Women Backpackers.* Oakland, CA: Shepherd Canyon Books, 2003.
———. *Camino Chronicle: Walking to Santiago.* Oakland, CA: Shepherd Canyon Books, 2006.
Alexander, Lawrence. *Through Hiker's Eyes: A Journey along the Appalachian Trail: Part One: Springer Mountain, Georgia to Harper's Ferry, West Virginia.* Jasper, AL: Trail Peddler Publishing, 2008.
———. *Through Hiker's Eyes: A Journey along the Appalachian Trail: Part Two: Katahdin Bound.* Jasper, AL: Trail Peddler Publishing, 2009.
Allen, Abe T. *An Unfinished Odyssey on the Appalachian Trail: A Memoir.* Waban, MA: 1stBooks, 2003.
Allnutt, Rick. *A Wildly Successful 200-Mile Hike: Lessons Learned from the Appalachian Trail.* Beavercreek, OH: Wayah Press, 2005.
Alt, Jeff. *A Walk for Sunshine: A 2,160 Mile Expedition for Charity on the Appalachian Trail.* Rev. ed. Cincinnati, OH: Dreams Shared Publications, 2007.
Altschuler, Stephen. *The Mindful Hiker: On the Trail to Find the Path.* Camarillo, CA: DeVorss, 2004.
Anderson, Larry. *Benton MacKaye: Conservationist, Planner, and Creator of the Appalachian Trail.* Baltimore, MD: Johns Hopkins University Press, 2002.

Atlanta Journal-Constitution staff et al. *Appalachian Adventure: From Georgia to Maine: A Spectacular Journey on the Great American Trail*. Atlanta, GA: Longstreet Press, 1995.

Austin, Mary Liz. *Appalachian Trail on My Mind: The Best of the Appalachian Trail in Words and Photographs*. Guilford, CT: Globe Pequot Press, 2003.

Ballard, Angela and Duffy. *A Blistered Kind of Love: One Couple's Trial by Trail*. Seattle, WA: Mountaineers Books, 2003.

Banfield, Walter M. *Metacomet-Monadnock Trail Guide*. 7th ed. Amherst, MA: Trails Committee of the Berkshire Chapter, Appalachian Mountain Club, 1991.

Bass, Rick. *The Deer Pasture*. College Station, TX: Texas A & M University Press, 1985. Paperback, New York: W.W. Norton, 1996.

———. *Winter: Notes from Montana*. Boston, MA: Houghton Mifflin/Seymour Lawrence, 1991.

———. *Why I Came West*. Boston, MA: Houghton Mifflin, 2008.

Bauer, Wolf, and Lynn Hyde. *Crags, Eddies & Riprap: The Sound Country Memoir of Wolf Bauer*. Seattle, WA: Northwest Passage Press, 2010.

Becerra, Cesar A., and Maud Dillingham. *Appalachian Trail Through Hiker Notebook*. Miami, FL: Becerra, 2004.

Berger, Karen, and Daniel R. Smith. *Where the Waters Divide: A 3,000-Mile Trek along America's Continental Divide*. New York: Harmony Books, 1993.

———. *Along the Pacific Crest Trail*. Englewood, CO: Westcliffe Publishers, 1998.

Berkshire Chapter, Appalachian Mountain Club, 1991. *Metacomet-Monadnock Trail Guide*. 10th ed. Amherst, MA: Trails Committee of the Berkshire Chapter, Appalachian Mountain Club, 2005.

Bischke, Scott. *Crossing Divides: A Couple's Story of Cancer, Hope, and Hiking Montana's Continental Divide*. Atlanta, GA: American Cancer Society, 2002.

Blanchard, Dennis R. *Three Hundred Zeroes: Lessons of the Heart on the Appalachian Trail*. [self-published]: CreateSpace.com, 2010.

Blaney, Melody, and Lindi Ullyart. *A Journey of Friendship: A Thru-Hike on the Appalachian Trail*. Marietta, OH: The River Press, 1997.

Booth, Alan. *The Roads to Sata: A 2,000-Mile Walk through Japan*. Tokyo: John Weatherhill, Inc., 1985.

Bouldrey, Brian. *Honorable Bandit: A Walk across Corsica*. Madison, WI: Terrace Books, 2007.

Brampton, Jesse. *Promises to Keep: An Australian on the Appalachian Trail*. New York: Bantam, 1993.

Brill, David. *As Far as the Eye Can See: Reflections of an Appalachian Trail Hiker.* 3rd ed. Harpers Ferry, WV: Appalachian Trail Conservancy, 2004.

Bryson, Bill. *A Walk in the Woods.* New York: Broadway, 1998.

Butler, Elias, and Tom Myers. *Grand Obsession, Harvey Butchart and the Exploration of Grand Canyon.* Flagstaff, AZ: Puma Press, 2007.

Campbell, Ffyona. *The Whole Story: A Walk around the World.* London: Orion, 1996.

Carr, Pam, and John Carr. *Follow the White Blazes from Georgia to Maine: British Hikers' Views of the Appalachian Trail.* York: Appalachian Walks UK, 1993.

Carver, Natasha. *Walking Down a Dream: Mexico to Canada on Foot.* Philadelphia, PA: Xlibris, 2002.

Chazin, Daniel D. *Appalachian Trail Data Book 2008.* 30th ed. Harpers Ferry, WV: Appalachian Trail Conservancy, 2007.

Chenowith, Lon. *Five Million Steps: Adventure along the Appalachian Trail.* Mustang, OK: Tate Publishing, 2009.

Cook, Scott. *Bend, Overall (A Guidebook about Hiking and Exploring the Central Oregon Area Surrounding Bend).* Sunriver, OR: Scott Cook, 2004.

Coplen, Jim. *The Wild Birds' Song: Hiking South on the Appalachian Trail.* South Bend, IN: American Bison, 1998.

Cornelius, Madelaine. *Katahdin (With Love): An Inspirational Journey.* Lookout Mountain, TN: Milton Publishing, 1991.

Curran, Jan D. *The Appalachian Trail: A Journey of Discovery.* Moore Haven, FL: Rainbow Books, 1991.

———. *The Appalachian Trail: Onward to Katahdin.* Moore Haven, FL: Rainbow Books, 1999.

Dawson, Paralee. *Living a Dream: Laughter, Pain and Life on the Appalachian Trail.* Murphy, NC: Gatewood Publishing, 2008.

Deeds, Jean. *There Are Mountains to Climb.* Indianapolis, IN: Silverwood Press, 1996.

Downer, Lesley. *On the Narrow Road: Journey into a Lost Japan.* New York: Summit Books, 1989.

Duane, Charlie. *Racing Light: The Soft Power of a Day's Walk.* Marion, MA: Stella's Dream, 2007.

Dykstra, Monica. *Alone in the Appalachians: A City Girl's Trek from Maine to the Gaspesie.* Vancouver, BC: Raincoast Books, 2002.

Ebbesmeyer, Curtis C. *Flotsametrics and the Floating World: How One Man's Obsession with Runaway Sneakers and Rubber Ducks Revolutionized Ocean Science.* New York: Smithsonian Books, 2009.

Eberhart, M. J. *Where Less the Path Is Worn: The Appalachian Mountains Trail, The Eastern Continental Trail.* Bloomingdale, OH: Thirsty Turtle Press, 2004.

———. *Ten Million Steps: Nimblewill Nomad's Epic 10-Month Trek from the Florida Keys to Quebec.* Birmingham, AL: Menasha Ridge Press, 2007.

Echols, Ray. *A Thru-Hiker's Heart: Tales of the Pacific Crest Trail.* Mariposa, CA: Tuolumne Press, 2009.

Egbert, Barbara. *Zero Days: The Real-life Adventure of Captain Bligh, Nellie Bly, and 10-year-old Scrambler on the Pacific Crest Trail.* Berkeley, CA: Wilderness Press, 2008.

Emblidge, David. *The Appalachian Trail Reader.* New York: Oxford University Press, 1996.

Espy, Gene. *The Trail of My Life: The Gene Espy Story.* Macon, GA: Indigo, 2008.

Eye, Herbert F. *An Eye on the Horizon: An Appalachian Trail Odyssey.* Grafton, OH: Ridgecrest Publishers, 1998.

Ferguson, Gary. *Walking down the Wild: A Journey through the Yellowstone Rockies.* New York: Simon & Schuster, 1993.

Fiennes, Ranulph. *Mind over Matter: The Epic Crossing of the Antarctic Continent.* New York: Delacorte Press, 1993.

Fletcher, Colin. *The Thousand Mile Summer in Desert and High Sierra.* Berkeley, CA: Howell-North Books, 1964.

———. *The Man Who Walked through Time: The Story of the First Trip Afoot through the Grand Canyon.* New York: Vintage Books, 1972 [c1967.]

———. *The Complete Walker IV.* New York: Knopf, 2002.

Flynn, Kevin, and Gary Gerhardt. *The Silent Brotherhood: Inside America's Racist Underground.* New York: Signet, 1990.

Fortunato, Donald J. *2,000 Miles on the Appalachian Trail.* Rev. ed. East Lyme, CT: Fortunato Books, 1991.

Gadola, Paul. *Lie in My Grave: Memories from an Appalachian Trail Hike.* Greenville, PA: Beaver Pond Publishing, 2001.

Garvey, Edward B. *Appalachian Hiker: Adventure of a Lifetime.* Oakton, VA: Appalachian Books, 1971.

———. *Appalachian Hiker II.* Oakton, VA: Appalachian Books, 1978.

———. *The New Appalachian Trail.* Birmingham, AL: Menasha Ridge Press, 1997.

Gill, Kathleen M. *Story Walking the Appalachian Trail.* Saratoga Springs, NY: Peckhaven Publishing, 2004.

Glyn, Patricia. *Footing with Sir Richard's Ghost.* Johannesburg, South Africa: Sharp Sharp Media, 2006.

Guilford, Eleanor. *One Hundred Mile Summers: Hiking the Pacific Coast Trail from Mexico to Canada.* Oakland, CA: Regent Press, 2005.

Hall, Adrienne. *A Journey North: One Woman's Story of Hiking the Appalachian Trail.* Boston, MA: Appalachian Mountain Club Books, 2001.

Harlin, John. "The Prophet of the PNT." *Backpacker Magazine*, May 2000.

Harrah, Andy. *Iron Toothpick: A Thru-Hiker Reveals Life, Legend and Oddities along the Appalachian Trail*. Oakton, VA: Rainmaker Publishing, 2006.

Hartley, Bob. *Care to Join Me?: Day by Day on the Appalachian Trail*. Victoria, B.C.: Trafford Publishing, 2003.

Haszonics, Joe J. *Trail Days: Thru-Hikers on the AT*. Margate, FL: Minuteman Press, 1998.

Hensley, Robie. *Appalachian Trail Journal*. Chuckey, TN: Robie Hensley, 1992.

Hills, Scot. *Trail Magic*. Maggie Valley, NC: Thirsty Turtle Press, 2005.

Hirsohn, Don. *The Appalachian Tale: The Adventures of the Poetry Man*. Canoga Park, CA: Canyon Publishing, 1986.

Hodgins, John J. *An Appalachian Trail Sketchbook: Sketches and Stories and People and Places and Six Years of Hiking*. Batavia, NY: Hodgins Printing, 1984.

Hodson, Peregrine. *Under a Sickle Moon: A Journey through Afghanistan*. New York: Traveler, 1987.

Holtel, Bob. *Soul, Sweat & Survival on the Pacific Crest Trail*. Belleville, Ontario: Essence Publishing, 2001.

Horton, David, and Rebekah Trittipoe. *A Quest for Adventure: David Horton's Conquest of the Appalachian Trail and the Trans-America Footrace*. Lynchburg, VA: Warwick House Publishing, 1997.

Hughes, M. E. *We're Off to See the Wilderness, the Wonderful Wilderness of Awes: A Hiker's 2000-Mile Adventure Journal of the Appalachian Trail*. Philadelphia, PA: Xlibris, 2005.

Hurlbert, Sandy, and Rodney Hurlbert. *Fred and Litefoot: Our Trek on the Appalachian Trail*. Estes Park, CO: Mountain Printery, 1995.

Irwin, Bill, and David McCasland. *Blind Courage*. Rev. ed. Harpers Ferry, WV: Appalachian Trail Conference, 1991.

Jardine, Ray. *Beyond Backpacking: Ray Jardine's Guide to Lightweight Hiking*. LaPine, OR: AdventureLore Press, 2000.

———. *Trail Life: Ray Jardine's Lightweight Backpacking*. LaPine, OR: AdventureLore Press, 2009.

Jenkins, Peter. *A Walk across America*. Boston: G. K. Hall, 1979.

Jensen, David, and Cynthia Jensen-Fugate,. *Through My Eyes: A Dream Fulfilled (the Appalachian Trail)*. Bloomington, IN: AuthorHouse, 2006.

Jordan, Ryan, ed. *Lightweight Backpacking and Camping: A Field Guide to Wilderness, Equipment, Technique, and Style*. Bozeman, MT: Beartooth Mountain Press, 2004.

Kerkeling, Hape. *I'm Off Then: My Journey along the Camino De Santiago*. New York: Free Press, 2009.

Leitschuh, Jan. *The Ordinary Adventurer: Hiking Vermont's Long Trail: A Primer for Baby Adventurers, and Other Musings on the Nature of the Journey*. Titusville, FL: Jerelyn Press, 2007.

Lemiux, Ferdinand. *Cinq Millions de Pas en Cinq Mois sur L'Appalachian Trail*. Bellevue, Saint-Romuald, Quebec: Les Éditions Sans Age, 1996.

Letcher, Elizabeth L., and Susan G. Letcher. *The Adventures of the Barefoot Sisters: Book 1: Southbounders*. Warner, NH: Flower Press, 2006.

———, and ———. *The Adventures of the Barefoot Sisters: Book 2: Northbounders*. Warner, NH: Flower Press, 2006.

Louv, Richard. *Last Child in the Woods: Saving Our Children from Nature-Deficit Disorder*. New York: Workman, 2005.

Lowther, Mic. *Walking North: A Family Hikes the Appalachian Trail*. 2nd ed. Seattle, WA: Elton-Wolf Publishing, 2001.

Luxenberg, Larry. *Walking the Appalachian Trail*. Harrisburg, PA: Stackpole Books, 1994.

McCaw, Bob. *The Thru-Hiker's Handbook*. 2011 edition. Conyers, GA: Center for Appalachian Trail Studies, 2011.

McDonnell, Jackie. *Yogi's CDT Handbook: Planning Tips and Town Guide*. Shawnee Mission, KS: Yogi's Books, 2006.

———. *Yogi's PCT Handbook*. Shawnee Mission, KS: Yogi's Books, 2004.

McKibben, Bill. *Wandering Home: A Long Walk across America's Most Hopeful Landscape: Vermont's Champlain Valley and New York's Adirondacks*. New York: Crown, 2005.

McKinney, Rick. *Dead Men Hike No Trails*. Bangor, ME: Booklocker, 2005.

Maroni, Bill. *When Straight Jacket Met Golden Sun: A Journey on the Appalachian Trail*. Philadelphia, PA: Xlibris, 2003.

Marshall, Ian. *Story Line: Exploring the Literature of the Appalachian Trail*. Charlottesville, VA: University Press of Virginia, 1998.

Martin, Danie. *Always Another Mountain: A Woman Hiking the Appalachian Trail from Springer Mountain to Mount Katahdin*. College Station, TX: Virtualbookworm.com POD Pub., 2005.

Mass, Leslie, ed. *Appalachian Trail Thru-Hikers' Companion 2009*. 16th ed. Harpers Ferry, WV: Appalachian Trail Conservancy, 2009.

Mass, Leslie. *In Beauty May She Walk: Hiking the Appalachian Trail At 60*. Jacksonville, FL: Rock Spring Press, 2005.

Meegan, George. *The Longest Walk: An Odyssey of the Human Spirit*. New York: Paragon House, 1989.

Meek, George. *Time for Everything: A Six-Year Adventure on the Appalachian Trail*. Vienna, VA: Potomac Appalachian Trail Club, 2003.

Miller, David. *AWOL on the Appalachian Trail*. 2nd ed. Livermore, CA: WingSpan Press, 2006.

———. *The A.T. Guide: A Handbook for Hiking the Appalachian Trail*. Titusville, FL: Jerelyn Press, 2010.

Molloy, Johnny. *Hiking the Florida Trail: 1,100 Miles, 78 Days, Two Pairs of Boots, and one Heck of an Adventure*. Gainesville: University Press of Florida, 2008.

Morland, Miles. *A Walk across France*. New York: Fawcett Columbine, 1992.

Motz, Randy, and Georgia Harris. *Solemates: Lessons on Life, Love & Marriage from the Appalachian Trail*. Germantown, MD: Qualtech Resource Group, 2008.

Mountain Marching Mamas. *It's Always Up: Memories of the Appalachian Trail*. Morrisville, NC: Lulu.com, 2007.

Mueser, Roland. *Long-Distance Hiking: Lessons from the Appalachian Trail*. Camden, ME: International Marine/Ragged Mountain Press, 1997.

Nelson, Jack. *Yak and Yo on the Appalachian Trail 1999*. Charlotte, NC: Preserving Memories, 2000.

Newell, Buddy. *You Won't Get to Maine unless You Walk in the Rain*. Littleton, NH: Bondcliff Books, 2002.

Newman, Steven M. *Worldwalk: An Incredible Tale of Adventure and Inspiration: One American's Four-Year Journey Alone and on Foot*. New York: William Morrow, 1989.

Otis, Stephen, and Colin Roberts. *A Road More or Less Traveled: Madcap Adventures along the Appalachian Trail*. Knoxville, TN: Sunnygold Books, 2008.

Peattie, Donald Culross. *A Natural History of North American Trees*. New York: Houghton Mifflin Harcourt, 2007.

Pern, Stephen. *The Great Divide: A Walk through America along the Continental Divide*. New York: Viking, 1988.

Pifher, Patrick J. *One Step at a Time: An Appalachian Trail Adventure*. Philadelphia, PA: Xlibiris, 2000.

Pittard, Patrick. *Bearfoot, A Northbounder: E-mails from the Appalachian Trail*. Birmingham, AL: Will Publishing, 2005.

Platt, Jay. *A Time to Walk: Life Lessons Learned on the Appalachian Trail*. Carterville, GA: Eagle Eye Publishing, 2000.

Porter, Winton. *Just Passin' Thru: A Vintage Store, the Appalachian Trail, and a Cast of Unforgettable Characters*. Birmingham, AL: Menasha Ridge Press, 2009.

Potterfield, Peter. *Classic Hikes of the World: 23 Breathtaking Treks*. New York: Norton, 2005.

Ray, Michelle, *How to Hike the AT: The Nitty Gritty Details of a Long Distance Trek*. Harrisburg, PA: Stackpole Books, 2009.

Reis, Rick. *3 Outta 4*. Fayetteville, NC: Old Mountain Press, 1999.

Richardson, James. *Once Upon a Climb: One Man's Journey on the Appalachian Trail*. San Antonio, TX: Booklocker Inc., 2005.

Ross, Cindy. *Scraping Heaven: A Family's Journey along the Continental Divide*. Camden, ME: Ragged Mountain Press, 2003.

———. *A Woman's Journey*. Harpers Ferry, WV: Appalachian Trail Conference (1990), 2009.

———, and Todd Gladfelter. *A Hiker's Companion: 12,000 Miles of Trail-Tested Wisdom*. Seattle, WA: Mountaineers, 1993.

———, and ———. *Kids in the Wild*. Seattle, WA: Mountaineers, 1995.

Rubin, Robert A. *On the Beaten Path: An Appalachian Pilgrimage*. New York: Lyons Press, 2001.

Runolfson, Kevin. *The Things You Find on the Appalachian Trail: A Memoir of Discovery, Endurance and a Lazy Dog*. Jefferson, NC: Mcfarland & Co., 2010.

Ryback, Eric. *The High Adventure of Eric Ryback: Canada to Mexico on Foot*. San Francisco, CA: Chronicle Books, 1971.

———. *The Ultimate Journey: Canada to Mexico down the Continental Divide*. San Francisco, CA: Chronicle Books, 1973.

Schaffer, Jeffrey P. *The Pacific Crest Trail: Volume 2: Oregon and Washington* Berkeley, CA: Wilderness Press, 1974.

———. *The Geomorphic Evolution of the Yosemite Valley and Sierra Nevada Landscapes: Solving the Riddles in the Rocks*. Berkeley, CA: Wilderness Press, 1997.

———, and Ben Schifrin. *The Pacific Crest Trail: Southern California, from the Mexican Border to Yosemite's Toulumne Meadows*. 6th ed. Berkeley, CA: Wilderness Press, 2003.

———, and ———. *The Pacific Crest Trail: Northern California, from Tuolumne Meadows to the Oregon Border*. 6th ed. Berkeley, CA: Wilderness Press, 2003.

———, ———, Thomas Winnett, and Ruby Johnson Jenkins. *The Pacific Crest Trail: Southern California*. Berkeley, CA: Wilderness Press, 2003.

———, and Andrew Selters. *The Pacific Crest Trail: Oregon & Washington, from California Border to the Canadian Border*. 7th ed. Berkeley, CA: Wilderness Press, 2004.

Schlimmer, E. *Thru-hiker's Guide to America: 25 Incredible Trails You Can Hike in One to Eight Weeks*. Camden, ME: Ragged Mountain Press, 2005.

Schmid, Jim. *American Trails Searchable Trails and Greenways Bibliography*. National Trails Training Partnership. http://www.americantrails.org/resources/info/bibliog.html. [Updated regularly.]

Schuette, Bill. *White Blaze Fever: Georgia to Maine on the Appalachian Trail*. College Station, TX: Virtualbookworm.com Publishing, 2003.

Schultz, Robin. *Sun Days: Hiking the Appalachian Trail*. Norman, OK: Poetry Around, 1989.

Scott, John. *To the Woods: A Journey along the Appalachian Trail*. Morrisville, NC: Lulu.com, 2006.

Sebald, G. G. *The Rings of Saturn*. Frankfurt am Main, Germany: Vito von Eichborn Gmbh & Co Verlag KG, 1995.

Setzer, Lynn. *A Season on the Appalachian Trail*. 2nd ed. Birmingham, AL: Menasha Ridge Press, 2001.

Shaffer, Earl V. *Walking with Spring: The First Thru-Hike of the Appalachian Trail*. Harpers Ferry, WV: Appalachian Trail Conference, 1983.

———. *Walking with Spring*. Harpers Ferry, WV: Appalachian Trail Conference, 1998.

———. *The Appalachian Trail: Calling Me Back to the Hills*. Photography by Bart Smith. Englewood, CO: Westcliffe, 2002.

Shepherd, Nancy. *My Own Hike: A Woman's Journey on the Appalachian Trail*. Morrisville, NC: Lulu.com, 2005.

Siefken, Kurt. *Mind, Muscle, and Mountain: A Six Month Adventure on the Appalachian Trail*. Longmont, CO: Mercury Worm Enterprises, 2004.

———. *Walking North: An Appalachian Trail Journal*. Longmont, CO: Mercury Worm Enterprises, 2004.

Sink, Chuck, and Norma Sink. *You Can't Get There by Sitting Here*. Bloomington, IN: AuthorHouse, 2008.

Solnit, Rebecca. *Wanderlust: A History of Walking*. New York: Viking Penguin, 2000.

———. *A Field Guide to Getting Lost*. New York: Viking Penguin, 2005.

Spearing, George. *Dances with Marmots, A Pacific Crest Trail Adventure*. Morrisville, NC: Lulu.com, 2005.

Stevenson, Andrew. *Kiwi Tracks: A New Zealand Journey*. Oakland, CA: Lonely Planet, 1999.

———. *Summer Light: A Walk across Norway*. Oakland, CA: Lonely Planet, 2002.

Stewart, Rory. *The Places in Between*. New York: Harcourt, 2006.

Strickland, Ron. *Ten Years of Congressional Review under the Wilderness Act of 1964 : Wilderness Classification through "Affirmative Action."* Dissertation (Ph. D.): Georgetown University, 1976.

———. *Pacific Northwest Trail Guide*. Seattle, WA: The Writing Works, 1984.

———. *Shank's Mare: A Compendium of Remarkable Walks*. New York: Paragon House, 1988.

———. *The Pacific Northwest Trail Guide.* 2nd Ed. Seattle, WA: Sasquatch Books, 2001.

———. *River Pigs and Cayuses.* Corvallis: Oregon State University Press, 2001.

———. *Whistlepunks and Geoducks.* Corvallis: Oregon State University Press, 2001.

Strickland, Winifred Gibson. *Obedience Class Instruction for Dogs: The Trainer's Manual.* New York: Macmillan, 1978.

———. *Expert Obedience Training for Dogs.* Indianapolis, IN: Howell Book House. 4th ed., 2003.

———, and James A. Moses. *The German Shepherd Today.* New York: Howell Book House, 1998.

Sullivan, William L. *Listening for Coyote: A Walk across Oregon's Wilderness.* New York: William Morrow, 1988. Paperback, Corvallis: Oregon State University Press, 2000.

Swan, David S. *Travels with Artsy and Twinkle Toes on the A.T.* Philadelphia, PA: Xlibris, 2004.

Talbot-Ponsonby, Spud. *Two Feet, Four Paws: The Girl Who Walked Her Dog 4,500 Miles.* Chichester, West Sussex, UK: Summersdale, 1996.

———. *Small Steps with Heavy Hooves: A Mother's Walk back to Health in the Highlands.* Chichester, West Sussex, UK: Summersdale, 1998.

Tapon, Francis. *Hike Your Own Hike: 7 Life Lessons from Backpacking across America.* Burlingame, CA: SonicTrek Press, 2006.

Tate, J. R. *Walkin' on the Happy Side of Misery.* Philadelphia, PA: Xlibris, 2001.

———. *Walkin' with the Ghost Whisperers: Lore and Legends of the Appalachian Trail.* Philadelphia, PA: Xlibris, 2006.

Tomaselli, Doris. *Ned Anderson: Connecticut's Appalachian Trailblazer & Small Town Renaissance Man.* Sherman, CT: Sherman Historical Society, 2009.

Tomlinson, Robert. *An American Adventure: Hiking the Appalachian Trail.* Chapel Hill, NC: Professional Press, 2003.

Townsend, Chris. *The Great Backpacking Adventure.* Sparkford, Somerset, UK: Oxford Illustrated Press, 1987.

———. *High Summer: Backpacking the Canadian Rockies.* Seattle, WA: Cloudcap, 1989.

———. *Crossing Arizona: A Solo Hike through the Sky Islands and Deserts of the Arizona Trail.* Woodstock, VT: Countryman Press, 2002.

Twitty, Mary. *The Dream Trail.* Verona, MO: Mary L. Twitty, 1997.

Viles, Brad Wayne. *Dreaming the Appalachian Trail: A Backpacking Novel.* Philadelphia, PA: Xlibris, 2006.

Wadness, Kenneth. *Sojourn in the Wilderness: A Seven Month Journey on the Appalachian Trail*. Prospect, KY: Harmony House Publishers, 1997.

Walker, Bill. *Skywalker: Close Encounters on the Appalachian Trail*. Macon, GA: Indigo Publishing Group, 2008.

Waterman, Laura, and Guy Waterman. *Forest and Crag: A History of Hiking, Trail Blazing, and Adventure in the Northeast Mountains*. Boston, MA: Appalachian Mountain Club, 1989, 2003.

Welch, Aaron. *Remember the Carrot: A Change of Pace on the Appalachian Trail*. Scotts Valley, CA: CreateSpace, 2008.

Weston, Walter. *Mountaineering and Exploring in the Japanese Alps*. London, UK: John Murray, 1896.

———. *Collected Works of Walter Weston*. London, UK: Ganesha Pub., 2001.

Whelden, Lynne. *Amazing Grace!: The Incredible Story of the Blind Appalachian Trail Thru-Hiker Bill Irwin*. VHS video. Canton, PA: Lynne Whelden Productions, 1992

White, Dan. *The Cactus Eaters: How I Lost My Mind—and Almost Found Myself—on the Pacific Crest Trail*. New York: Harper Perennial, 2008.

Wilson, Brandon. *Yak Butter Blues: A Tibetan Trek of Faith*. Paia, HI: Pilgrim's Tales, 2004.

———. *Along the Templar Trail: Seven Million Steps for Peace*. Paia, HI: Pilgrim's Tales, 2008.

———. *Over the Top & Back Again: Hiking X the Alps*. Paia, HI: Pilgrim's Tales, 2010.

Winters, Kelly. *Walking Home: A Woman's Pilgrimage on the Appalachian Trail*. Los Angeles, CA: Alyson Books, 2001.

Wolfe, Ellen. *Walking the Dream*. Cookeville, TN: One Step Press, 1999.

Wren, Christopher S. *Walking to Vermont: From Times Square into the Green Mountains—A Homeward Adventure*. New York: Simon & Schuster, 2004.

Young, Joan H. *North Country Cache: Adventures on a National Scenic Trail*. Scottville, MI: Books Leaving Footprints, 2005.

Zug, James. *American Traveler: The Life and Adventures of John Ledyard, the Man Who Dreamed of Walking the World*. New York: Basic Books, 2005.

Index